Still: *Mother Joan of the Angels*

RELIGION IN THE CINEMA
by Ivan Butler

In the same series,
produced by THE TANTIVY PRESS
and edited by Peter Cowie:

Religion in the Cinema

by IVAN BUTLER

THE INTERNATIONAL FILM GUIDE SERIES

A. S. BARNES & CO., NEW YORK

A. ZWEMMER LIMITED, LONDON

Acknowledgements

I SHOULD LIKE TO EXPRESS my thanks to the staff of the British Film Institute Reference Department for their ever willing and efficient help; to Peter Cowie and Allen Eyles for much helpful advice; and particularly to the Rev. John A. V. Burke and the Rev. A. S. Hopkinson for kindly reading through the typescript, for correcting some clerical errors, and, while they are in no way responsible for opinions expressed in the text, for suggesting a number of interesting details which I have gladly incorporated. My thanks are also due to Arthur Lomas for the information given in the Appendix.

My thanks also to the following for permission to reproduce the stills: AB Svensk Filmindustri; Cinedistri Limitada, Brazil; Columbia; Compton; Connoisseur; Contemporary; Gala; Maurice Hatton; Miracle; Paramount; Polish Cultural Institute; Rank; Twentieth-Century Fox; United Artists; Warner Pathé.

COVER STILLS
Front and back (top): *The Greatest Story Ever Told* (Courtesy of United Artists) (Max von Sydow as Jesus). Black and white still (back) from *Dante's Inferno*.

FIRST PUBLISHED 1969
Copyright © 1969 by Ivan Butler
Library of Congress Catalog Card No. 69–14897

SBN 302–02003–9 (U.K.)

SBN 498–07417–X (U.S.A.)

Printed in the United States of America

Contents

Introduction

THIS BOOK IS INTENDED as a survey of the treatment of Biblical history and Christian practice in the commercial film, from the point of view of a layman, a study of religion in films rather than films in religion. I have endeavoured to approach the subject as objectively and in as wide a sense as possible. Chapters are included on anti-religious films, and on the obverse side such as witchcraft and Satanic rites.

Selecting the most convenient method of classification has presented a few problems, and inevitably some of the chapter divisions may seem arbitrary. I have in general placed real people under the designation by which they are most popularly known. For example, Francis of Assisi appears in the chapter on Saints rather than that on Monks, Vincent de Paul under Priests rather than Saints. In each chapter I have in general observed a roughly chronological order, but when it seemed convenient have kept together films which have certain points in common, e.g. those on St. Joan, or those concerned with miracles of the Virgin Mary. The Index at the end of the book will enable any particular film to be quickly traced. English titles of foreign films have been used except in cases where the foreign title is much better known.

Obviously, in a book of this length on so large a subject, there is not room for extended analyses of particular films. Many excellent detailed examinations already exist and a selection will be found in the Bibliography. Symbol-searching and hidden-significance-hunting are great fun (and apparently quite profitable too), even if they sometimes call to mind Beethoven's supposed exclamation on reading the late Sir Donald Francis Tovey's wonderful essays in musical analysis:

Left: KING OF KINGS (1961)

"Good God, did I really mean all that?" Quite understandably, films concerned with religion or metaphysics, particularly if they are allegorical in form, offer more opportunities than most for such fascinating and rewarding excavations. If paradoxical conclusions can be reached, all the merrier. Bresson is now a heretic, Buñuel a concealed Catholic, Bergman . . . ? Some years ago there was a poster to be found in many Underground lifts, put up by a religious body. It illustrated a tube-traveller's astonishment at seeing the transverse beams supporting the roof of the lift, and his awed realisation that "we all stand under the Sign of the Cross"—a symbolic discovery which must have astounded the constructors of the lift as much as Sir Francis astounded Beethoven. It may, I think, be fairly suggested that film analyses (my own, no doubt, among them— it's an infectious joy) sometimes tend to overlook the element of chance.

Clearly not every film containing a priest, monk, church, missionary, hermit, etc. can (or should) be mentioned. I have in the main selected those whose religious function has some definite bearing on the story, even if their actual part in the film may be smaller than others which have been left out. Limitations of space have also meant the omission of numerous films dealing with ethical problems (war and peace, black and white, the clash of loyalties) which, though they may well be considered "religious" in the broadest sense, confine their significance to this world: and also of such momentary experiences of worship as (at one end) the "heavenly choir" fade-outs, and (at the other) the deeply moving utterance of the Lord's Prayer at the close of the submarine film *Morning Departure*. However, I have tried to be inclusive rather than exclusive, and hope that the result is a reasonably complete handbook of the more interesting commercial films concerned wholly or in part with religion.

1. Bible Stories and Biblical Blockbusters; Early Christians; Crusades

THE BIBLE

FILM-MAKERS were quick off the mark in realising the attractions of the religion-cum-sex formula, and as early as 1903 one of the founders of the French cinema, Ferdinand Zecca, having already made a *Prodigal Son* in 1901, directed what is probably the first version of *Samson and Delilah*. Pathé followed with a *Prodigal Son* in 1907 and a *Samson and Delilah* ("ending with his entrance into Paradise") in 1908. The first Biblical murder story appeared in 1905 with Méliès's *Justice and Vengeance Pursuing Crime* (after Proud'hon) which seems—from an extant still showing one skin-clad man fleeing across the rocks from the body of another, pursued by determined-looking angels—to have been inspired by Cain and Abel. In the year 1909 the American Vitagraph Company set out a Biblical feast consisting of a *Jephthah's Daughter*, a *Salome*, a *Judgment of Solomon* ("Grand Biblical Reel for Sunday Shows"), and a *Saul and David*. The latter was noted as a novelty in that the characters were introduced "with individual pictures before the commencement of the Story proper." In 1910 the Company followed these up with a five-reel *Life of Moses*. An Italian film on Herodias (*Erodiade*) appeared in 1912 with Suzanne de Labroy in the title role.

1913 saw what might now be called the first Biblical blockbuster—D. W. Griffith's *Judith of Bethulia*. This version of the Apocrypha story was made in Chatsworth, California, on a spectacular scale and is the first flowering of the Griffith genius, revealing already his skill in handling large vistas without losing individual interests. The cast includes most of the later Griffith repertory—Blanche Sweet, Henry B. Walthall, Robert

Nazimova . . . . stylistic SALOME with bubbles (1922).

Harron, Mae Marsh and, in a small part, Lillian Gish. Other pre-war Bible stories included the Italian *Maccabees*, from Cines; Pathé's *David and Goliath;* the American Thanhouser's *Joseph in the Land of Egypt* with James Cruze, later noted as a director; and Universal's *Samson* with J. Warren Kerrigan as Samson and Mayme Kelso as Delilah, for which an advance in admission prices was recommended.

The First World War years seem to have had an understandably restraining influence on Biblical film-making, but in 1918 Theda Bara's *Salome* appeared, directed by J. Gordon

10

Edwards, with Miss Bara dripping pearls prodigally as she vamps a buxom John the Baptist (Albert Roscoe) who seems to thrive remarkably well on his diet of locusts and wild honey. A far more interesting *Salome,* which startles even today, is that of Nazimova in 1922, directed by Charles Bryant. The *décor* and costumes were based on the drawings of Aubrey Beardsley by Natasha Rambova, wife of Rudolph Valentino, and the whole presentation was highly stylised. It was also considered highly scandalous. Nazimova produced the film herself and lost heavily on the venture. Despite many extravagances, it has a beauty and fascination which can still hold today, and is worth the demands it may make on the sympathetic understanding of a present-day audience. Nazimova, with her boyish figure and fantastically bewigged head (wigs ranging from flaxen bob to pearl bobbins), miraculously suggests the youth of the daughter of Herodias—yet she was forty-three at the time. Nigel de Brulier, though somewhat clean for an imprisoned prophet, looks suitably wasted by the fire of fanaticism. Mitchell Lewis is an oilily decadent Herod, and Rose Dione, the accomplished character actress who later played the motherly matron in Browning's *Freaks,* is Herodias. As might have been expected, contemporary criticism varied wildly. On one hand, the film was listed among the six best of the year, on another Nazimova was unkindly described as a "petulant little princess with a Freudian complex and a headdress of glass bubbles." Highly artificial, sometimes ludicrous, it is nevertheless beautiful and astonishing, and a constant pleasure to watch.

Another *Samson and Delilah* appeared in 1922, directed in Austria by Alexander Korda, and the *Queen of Sheba* arrived the same year in the person of Betty Blythe. This was directed by J. Gordon Edwards, who had been responsible for Theda Bara's *Salome.* Betty Blythe was at the time in the process of replacing Miss Bara as chief vamp at the Fox studios, and dripped even more pearls, if little else. Her costumes, in fact, as preserved in available stills, have to be seen to be believed. She was, however, an actress of considerable personality. Fritz Leiber was the somewhat submerged Solomon. He was beardless because, in the view of the director, "no motion picture audience would stand for Sheba falling in love with a set of whiskers." The film was described contemporarily as the love romance of the most beautiful woman the world had ever known.

The following year saw a major spectacle by the most famous epic-builder of them all. It is not always remembered, however, that the Biblical part of Cecil B. DeMille's 1923 *The Ten Commandments* is only a prologue to introduce and point the moral of a modern story, thus following a form he had already used in such films as *Male and Female* and *Manslaughter*. The modern story, concerning two brothers, one of whom kept the Commandments while the other broke them and thereby brought tragedy on himself and his family, is itself spectacular. Allowing for the melodramatics of the period, and a slight straining to get all the commandments into the framework of the story, it holds plenty of interest and excitement, and is aided by excellent performances from Richard Dix (one of the few actors able to make "goodness" neither boring nor smug), Rod la Rocque and Edythe Chapman. Only Nita Naldi as the conventional vamp remained firmly entrenched in the ludicrous. It is interesting to note that the disease which the young profligate contracted from her, and on account of which he killed her, was leprosy—the vamp having escaped from a colony: today such details would doubtless be more simply, and more realistically, arranged. The climax was the collapse of a half-finished cathedral which the bad brother had been constructing with poor quality sustaining fibres (despite the warnings of the good Mr. Dix), in order to realise a greater profit. In its fall, the building crushes their mother to death. This scene, with the percussion section of the large cinema orchestra going full out while the blocks of cement cracked and crashed until there remained only the stone tablet (the same shape as that Moses received on Sinai) bearing the words THOU SHALT NOT STEAL in huge Gothic lettering and looming significantly over the cringing human figures, was great stuff in its day. The Biblical section of the film, telling the story of the Exodus and the giving of the Commandments to Moses, naturally invites comparison with DeMille's 1956 re-make. Despite the technical improvements,

Pagan revelry—DeMille style:
THE TEN COMMANDMENTS (1956)

the fact that it was largely filmed on actual location, and the enormously increased length and cost of the whole thing, the later version has by no means all the advantages. The comparative brevity of the 1923 film meant that there was no need to pad it out with a fictitious (and tedious) love story involving "Prince" Moses, a hereditary Egyptian princess, and the Pharaoh's son. DeMille defends these innovations in his autobiography, claiming that research shows that at least they *could* have occurred—but it would have been better for the first part of his film if they hadn't. The 1923 orgy is more exciting than the comparatively restrained goings-on around the 1956 Golden Calf. The loss of silence may have been partly responsible here—chatter is apt to slow down orgiastic riotings. Above all, Charlton Heston's Moses, dignified, sympathetic and at times powerful though it is, does not achieve the majestic stature of Theodore Roberts. Even in the still photographs his long, windswept beard and hair, blazing eyes and width of gesture, convey something of the prophetic fire of the Biblical Leader of his people which is missing from the more modern approach of Heston. The parting of the Red Sea, admittedly, benefited greatly from improved techniques in the 1956 version, earning for the special effects department under John Fulton a well-deserved Oscar, but on the whole the later film seems weighed down with a heavy solemnity which the old, briefer prologue avoided, while yet creating a sense of awe and grandeur by simpler means. DeMille has full and interesting accounts of the making of both pictures in his autobiography, but refuses to divulge the secret of the Red Sea partings in either the first version (filmed

Left, top: Moses (1923), Theodore Roberts
Below: Moses (1956), Charlton Heston
—from DeMille's two versions of
THE TEN COMMANDMENTS.

15

at Guadalupe, California) or the second (at Abu Rawash, the Red Sea itself, and in the studio). He also refrains "from reverence" from giving the name of the actor who spoke the words of God in the 1956 film while delivering the Commandments—elsewhere Heston's own voice is used. In addition he makes confusion worse confounded by countering the critics who objected to the use of the name Princess Nefretiri (or Nefertiti) as inaccurate, by pointing out that there were actually two royal personages, Queens Nefretiti and Nefertiri, who lived 150 years apart. Anne Baxter presumably plays an amalgam of the two (or four), but in any case does not do it very well.

Paramount's *The Wanderer* (1925, *dir*. Raoul Walsh) is a somewhat extravagant rendering of the parable of the Prodigal Son, redeemed largely by the sincerity of William Collier Jnr., and the beauty of the Swedish actress Greta Nissen. As often, the quiet, Palestinian home-life scenes are much more convincing than those of Biblical high life. A long-haired and bearded Wallace Beery looks memorably uncomfortable wooing the langorous Miss Nissen, while clad in a gaudy helmet and a suit of armour which might have pleased Field-Marshal Goering.

Noah's Ark (Warner Brothers, 1930) had the misfortune to hit the hybrid "part-talkie" period. It belongs to the modern-story-with-Biblical-flashback family and, though enthusiastically received at the time, leaves little impression on the memory. George O'Brien starred with Dolores Costello. Myrna Loy appeared in a minor part. Noah Beery was also in the cast, but not, I think, as his namesake in the flood story. A Beery Noah would, I imagine, have remained in the mind.

The Green Pastures (1936, *dir*. Marc Connelly, William Keighley) is a filming of the enormously successful stage play in which stories from the Old Testament are visualised in

Negro Heaven: Rex Ingram as De Lawd in THE GREEN PASTURES

the minds of Negro children as they are taught in Sunday school by an old preacher. Heaven is a perpetual fish-fry in a park; God a kindly grizzled Negro gentleman in a far from new frock coat, able to work miracles but often uncertain as how best to run his troublesome new creation, earth. Coloured angels, in white robes obviously often washed and of inexpensive material, fly around on clouds or cluster along the walls of the Heavenly park to look down on the world with evident and kindly interest. "De Lawd's" Holy of Holies is a small office dominated by a battered rolltop desk and looked after by garrulous char-angels. His right-hand man, Gabriel, has to be warned against the temptation to blow his trumpet prematurely. From time to time God goes along to see how things are progressing on his earth, and is none too pleased at what he finds. Adam's fall, Cain and Abel, the Flood (with preacher Noah trying to persuade De Lawd to let him take into the Ark an extra keg of whisky "for snake bite")—all these and others are enacted as a Negro child might imagine them. Miraculously the pitfalls of whimsy are avoided for nine-tenths of the way. Modern criticism may look for an attitude of condescension towards coloured people in such a film, but this is hindsight thinking. No *intention* of such an attitude is apparent, and, as always, a film must be judged in the context of its time. Only at the end, when God through man glorifies conquest with guns and bayonets, does it become unaccept-able, in its period as much as in the present nuclear-conscious age. Here the vengeful old Jehovah rears his angry head, entirely inconsistent with the preachings of the stern but gentle old man, and the film loses its grip. Rex Ingram, doubling God and the man He made in His own image, is dignified, kindly, humorous, often worried, sometimes stern, always compassionate. "Even bein' God," he remarks, "ain't no bed of roses."

It was obvious that DeMille would one day have a shot at *Samson and Delilah*. The result, appearing in 1949, is sur-prisingly tame. Undoubtedly he was hampered by the casting of Hedy Lamarr as Delilah—a simpering, colourless, almost clinically asexual portrayal of probably the sexiest character in history. Victor Mature is unimpressive for a large part of the time, but attains some dignity and even grandeur in mis-fortune. The film has its moments—a DeMille epic could scarcely avoid doing so, but as Simon Harcourt-Smith points out, some of the moments of highest drama in the Bible story are inexplicably omitted, such as the fact that it was twice revealed to Samson that Delilah was out to ensnare him, and even so he is unable to break her spell. DeMille defends the film vigorously in his book, but with its reliance on cheap

18

thrills and scenes of sadism it is a disappointment. The most that can be said is that when DeMille fails, he fails spectacularly.

After Samson and Delilah, *David and Bathsheba*, directed by Henry King in 1951—a courageous attempt at a Bible story in a non-DeMille style, which, in doing away with the extravagances, does away also, alas, with most of the excitement and panache. The story is watered down in order to minimise David's thoroughly reprehensible behaviour, and the result is merely dull. Gregory Peck does what he can with his material, and on one or two occasions rises well above it, but Susan Hayward's Bathsheba seems hardly worth all the trouble. Only the veteran Francis X. Bushman as Saul has any real stature. David's battle with Goliath is shown in flashback but does not help matters much. Indeed, one is left in the end rather wishing Goliath had won. Resulting events might have been more exciting, at any rate.

The Queen of Sheba arrives again in 1952, from Italy this time, directed by Pietro Francisci. Gino Cervi, an odd choice, is Solomon, and Leonora Ruffo the Queen. Solomon's wisdom is demonstrated in the customary way (baby-dividing, etc.) and the film is fairly spectacular but not much else.

Although not strictly a Bible story, the Swedish *Barabbas* (1952) may be included here. Directed by Alf Sjöberg, it recounts the imaginary fate of the robber who is pardoned that Jesus Christ might take his place on the Cross. It was shot in Israel and Italy and, according to Peter Cowie (in his *Swedish Cinema*) is "ponderous in execution but contains a dignified performance by Ulf Palme." The story is based on a novel by Pär Lagerkvist. In 1961 another version came from Italy, directed, with English dialogue, by Richard Fleischer. Both films follow the main events of the novel: the imprisonment of Barabbas in the copper (or sulphur) mines of Sicily, his struggles to come to terms with the new religion, his involvement in the burning of Rome and his final death by crucifixion in the arena. But whereas the Swedish film concentrated on one man's personal dilemma and found in it parallels to our present day perplexities, the large-scale Italian version turned the story into the usual pseudo-religious spectacle with lashings of cruelty and death, much competently handled violent action in the arena sequences, but nothing below the surface.

In 1953 the *Sins of Jezebel* were enacted in America by Paulette Goddard under the direction of Reginald Le Borg. The choice of actresses to portray these more than life-size Bible characters never ceases to amaze, if not amuse. The film is a pale and damp account of the fiery, blood-curdling events, and makes one wonder why criticism so often belabours DeMille. Much the same might be said about another American offering of the same year, Rita Hayworth's *Salome,* which plumbs depths of vulgarity and inanity never reached by the Master at his wonderful worst. The scenario is a travesty of the Bible story, with Salome converted by John the Baptist and secretly intending to demand his release before dropping her final veil. However, nobody is interested, so Salome, after the arrival of the severed head, tells Herod and Herodias she wants nothing more to do with them and flounces off (with her lover) to listen to the Sermon on the Mount. Production of the film was continuously disturbed, apparently, by differences between Miss Hayworth and the head of Columbia, Harry Cohn. Unfortunately the disagreements were not severe enough to result in the whole project being abandoned.

The Prodigal (1955, *dir.* Richard Thorpe) is another elaboration (to put it mildly) of the adventures of the erring son, but lacks the sincerity and atmosphere of the more modest silent version, *The Wanderer.* The parable is vastly expanded.

and embellished: among other events the prodigal son falls in love with a pagan princess. Not much harm in this—after all *something* must have been going on during all that time of riotous living, but Edmund Purdom awakens neither the sympathy nor the interest that Buster Collier aroused, and dialogue, as so often before in these cases, does its fell work in the shattering of illusion.

A Mexican film on the creation of Man ought to have proved interesting, but unfortunately Alberto Gout's *Adam and Eve* (1956) becomes merely a reverent adventure story of a young couple battling against the elements (after the Fall) and, incredibly, returning repentant to Eden when they have had enough. One is left wondering what happens in History thereafter, the Book being apparently closed. Described by a critic as the first religious nudist film, it suffers more than usually from the characters' leaping by lucky chance from one concealing bush to another, inevitably awakening unfortunate (and frustrated) interest in what will happen when there comes an unbridgeable gap. Dialogue, sensibly, is absent throughout. Eve, not so sensibly, is portrayed by the Miss Universe of the period.

The Queen of Sheba's most recent visit, in *Solomon and Sheba* (1959, *dir.* King Vidor) is her best, and indeed one of the most acceptable of the Biblical epics. It was filmed in Spain on an immense and costly scale. It has, of course, its extravagances—the Queen's portable living quarters, for instance, which when folded and stowed would have filled a fleet of pantechnicons and remind one irresistibly of the Greatest Show on Earth. However, it is handled on the whole with admirable restraint. It is almost unfailingly pleasant to look at, particularly as regards the Palace interiors and the convincing representations of the "Palestinian" countryside. The shots of Solomon's Temple reproduce very faithfully the reconstructions of archaeologists. It is all "picture-book Bible," of course, but in this respect no more reprehensible than dozens of highly esteemed paintings. Dialogue, apart from a few unfortunate lines ("We've all felt the effect of the past few days"), is generally adequate and at times very effective. The story built around the visit is at least acceptable. The big climaxes—particularly the blinding of the enemy armies with sun-reflecting shields so that they charge headlong into a ravine—are splendidly exciting. Gina Lollobrigida is a sonsy Sheba with, for once, something of oriental regality, even in her tantrums. Yul Brynner, replacing Tyrone Power, is dignified and persuasive as Solomon, and Finlay Currie towers over all in his brief scenes as the dying David, an awe-inspiring and moving portrayal of an ancient patriarch. But what really makes this film stand out from its kind is that Vidor does manage to convey, for a few short moments, a real feeling of the Fear of God—the shadow of an Almighty Presence above the little seething turmoil of human beings. It is a feeling which DeMille also manages fleetingly to arouse, and which excuses him much.

The Italian *David and Goliath* of the same year (*dir.* Richard Pottier, Ferdinandi Baldi) is, by contrast, an overblown affair, noteworthy only for the appearance of Orson Welles as Saul. The film suffers further from being vilely dubbed for the English (or American) victim. Dubbing—in the form of slapping one language on to the lip movements of another—is the most destructive insult that can be offered to any film. No film can survive it, and no film is bad enough to deserve it. Films with religious themes suffer no more or less than others, but the vile procedure needs to be fought on every possible occasion.

Another Italian picture of the same year, *Herod the Great*, also dubbed, deals with the decline and eventual insanity of

Herod of Judea in the years before and just after the birth of Christ. The result is a hodge-podge of inaccuracies, with the unhappy Herod played by an even unhappier Edmund Purdom.

Esther and the King (1960) an Italo-American venture directed by Raoul Walsh, adheres fairly closely to the Bible story—and in fact the reason for Ahasueras the King seeking a new wife, Queen Vashti's infidelity, is more understandable than his rather silly behaviour in the original. There are some handsome moments of military spectacle, but not much else. Esther's story still awaits the stirring film which could be created from it. Again from Italy—having a Biblical field-day at this period—*Sold into Egypt* (*dir.* Luciano Ricci, Irving Rapper) recounts the story of Joseph, Potiphar and his wife, the dream of the seven fat and seven lean kine, and the ensuing famine. The film is unsensational but rather flat. In a mainly Italian (dubbed) cast, Finlay Currie (splendid David of *Solomon and Sheba*) again stands out in the relatively small role of Jacob. Robert Morley looks as surprised as we are to find himself as Potiphar, but carries it off with aplomb.

It is unfair, perhaps, to criticise the English version of Robert Aldrich's Italo-French *Sodom and Gomorrah* (1961) because the director states (in *Movie* number 6) that in at least one vital respect censorship cuts have damaged its entire structure. The original apparently enlarged on the sins of the Cities of the Plain, which as things are seem scarcely to have deserved the fearful punishment meted out to them. Apart from some exciting action shots the existing film is insipid, with Stewart Granger an unimpressive Lot and Anouk Aimée a very Twentieth century Queen of Sodom—is it in a spirit of extreme subtlety that the former King Bera of Sodom is here designated Queen Bera? The film ends with the not very convincing salification of Ildith, Lot's slave-girl wife, after his daughters have been used as pawns in a melodramatic game of villainous violation and paternal vengeance.

Saul and David (1965, *dir.* Marcello Baldi), from Italy once more, is a straightforward picturisation of the Biblical events —Samuel, the election of Saul as king, David and Goliath, war with the Philistines, death of Saul, David as king—none of it particularly foolish, or impressive.

The Bible—In the Beginning (1966, *dir.* John Huston) is all that eventuated from an enormous project to film the Old Testament more or less complete, with a heavily impressive list of directors and stars to be involved. Perhaps because of the high expectations aroused, the fragment (in spite of its three hours' length, it really is only a fragment) has received some harsh criticism, not all of it deserved. The film is a representation, not an interpretation, and on this level there is quite a lot to please. The Creation, admittedly, is unimpressive stuff (Hammer's *One Million Years B.C.* was much better), consisting as it does of superimposed smudgy eruptions of land and sea. The greenery-yallery Garden of Eden, however, is really rather attractive—a pleasant place for a hot afternoon. Adam and Eve have been attacked because they resemble modern American college students. But why not? They *were* a young couple, and throughout the ages painters and sculptors have represented the myths of religion in the likeness of their own period and place. Nobody holds it against Raphael that his Madonnas are Fifteenth century Italian matrons. The behind-bush-dodging again brings to mind

Right: THE BIBLE—IN THE BEGINNING

Top left: the disobedient Eve (Ulla Bergryd) hears the angry voice of God. Top right: Abel (Franco Nero) lies slain and Cain (Richard Harris) cries out, "Am I my brother's keeper?" Lower left: Abraham (George C. Scott) lifts his son Isaac (Alberto Lucatoni) in preparation for the sacrifice. Lower right: Abraham raises the knife over Isaac.

the conventional "nudie," but any alternative would have been cut—and anyway it is quite unobtrusively contrived in this case. The couple's facial expressions are mostly of blank wonder—but primeval innocence probably was fairly lacking in expression, and in fact Eve's fall into temptation is quite impressively done. The Cain and Abel sequence contains one magnificent long shot, and the Tower of Babel is a fine set—both episodes brief enough to avoid becoming tedious. Noah's Ark, with Huston himself as Noah, is generally exempted from critical condemnation, but the story of the Flood is almost infallible. Actually, some of the animal superimposition shots are poor, the inside of the Ark looks much too big for the outside, and Huston himself is a slight disappointment, Fry's script being probably to blame here. Still, there is a nice shot of him helping along one tardy tortoise as the rains swell, and the flood itself is magnificent.

By far the longest section of the film deals with Abraham, Sarah, Hagar, Isaac, Lot and company, and here, it must be admitted, in spite of George C. Scott's impressive patriarch, events do begin to weigh heavily. Even so, the Sarah-Hagar situation is quite moving, largely owing to Ava Gardner's moving performance—though it would probably have been more so had the film been a silent one and some banal dialogue avoided thereby. There are some notably exciting battle scenes lit by fitful fire, and the brief glimpse of Sodom and Gomorrah more effectively suggests nasty goings-on than more elaborate productions have achieved. Lot's flight, in flaming colour, is thrilling, though the atomic bomb fire and brimstone link-up is a bit obvious. The most serious, or ludicrous, misjudgment is the casting of Peter O'Toole as three angels at once. The appearance of his face, first under one cowl then under another, as they (he) all squat in a row reminds the viewer of nothing so much as a fairground game of Spot-the-

THE BIBLE—
IN THE BEGINNING:
the first skyscraper,
Nimrod's Tower of Babel.

Lady. The American commentary is on the whole discreet and acceptable, despite some oddities of accentuation such as: "In sorrow shalt thou bring forth *children*," as if she might have been expecting to give birth to something else.

EARLY CHRISTIANS

The two most famous Christians-to-the-Lions stories in the cinema are *Quo Vadis?* and *The Sign of the Cross.* There is a tradition that St. Peter, on his way from Rome during the persecution of the Christians under Nero, met Jesus going towards the City. "Quo vadis, Domine?" he asked—Whither goest thou, Lord? Jesus replied: "If you leave my people, I must return to be crucified again." Peter thereupon turned back. From this legend Henry Sienkiewicz developed his famous novel. The first film version was made by Zecca for Pathé in 1901, and the same company produced a second in 1908. It was given the full treatment by Italy under the direction of Enrico Guazzoni in 1913. He also wrote the script, and the production was considered remarkable at the time for the fluid handling of its enormous crowd scenes, its real lions, its chariot race, its burning of Rome, and its bestial Nero in Amelia Cattaneo. The film's *décor* was inspired by frescoes and paintings and won the approval of the sculptor Rodin, while the athletic hero (variously named as Mario Castellano and Bruto Castellani) was acclaimed for his prowess by King George V.

The 1924 version, an Italo-German production, was directed by Gabrielle d'Annunzio jointly with George Jacoby—another vast spectacle, with a heavily Teutonic Nero in Emil Jannings. Wearing an extraordinary wig resembling a sort of furry tea-cosy, he nevertheless manages to dominate the proceedings with a powerful if self-indulgent performance, but the film as a whole remains in the memory as a stodgy pudding, and the poetic quality which seems to have distinguished the early version is largely missing here. Its cost was enormous, and it lost money heavily. A third equally elaborate re-make was produced in 1951 (*dir.* Mervyn LeRoy) in the Italian Cinecittà studios, taking two years to complete. It included a lengthy sermon by St. Peter (Finlay Currie) intercut with flashbacks of the gospel story in the form of tableaux. Flabby dialogue worked its usual deadly effect on pseudo-historical spectacle, and even Peter Ustinov's pansy Nero failed to lighten the proceedings.

An early film version of Wilson Barrett's play *The Sign of the Cross* was made by W. Haggar in Great Britain in 1897, and a second by Adolph Zukor in 1914 with Dustin Farnum in the lead. The famous DeMille epic came out in 1932 (re-issued in 1946 with a ridiculous prologue about American air force pilots flying over the Open City), and it is still remembered with affection and revived with success. For so early a "talkie" it is astonishingly lively, despite some platitudinous religious discussions, and much of it has the flair of DeMille at his best. Wisely, he gives the melodramatics of the hoary old play full rein. Elissa Landi is a beautiful but colourless

DeMille's THE SIGN OF THE CROSS: Christian victim (Elissa Landi) at right, Roman officer (Fredric March) at left

Christian victim, and Fredric March does more than could be expected with the Roman officer who is converted to Christianity (or should it be, to Elissa?) and joins hands with her to meet a martyr's death. The villains, however, as so often, come out best. Claudette Colbert is a seductive and (in one scene literally) milky Poppaea, and Charles Laughton's Nero, if not a thing of beauty, is at least a joy for ever. His words "delicious debauchery," dripped from his lips with true Laughton gusto, became a catch-phrase. Nor must it be forgotten that he invested the character with a genuine pathos. DeMille's book referred to above contains an entertaining account of the making of this film also, and of the Catholic opposition with which parts of it were met.

Gabriel Pascal's production of *Androcles and the Lion* (1952, *dir.* Chester Erskine) is an inflated version of Shaw's light comedy about the slave who extracted the thorn from a lion's paw and was later greeted with affection by the animal on being thrown to it in the arena. The Shavian wit and wisdom which embellished the old tale of Aulus Gellius is smothered and the film becomes just another minor spectacle. *The Robe* (1953, *dir.* Henry Koster) deals with the influence of Christ's robe on the mind of a Roman Officer (Richard Burton), who wins it at the dice game supposed to have taken place among the guards at the Crucifixion. He passes the garment on to his Christian slave but is unable to escape its grip on his imagination. The robe, in fact, becomes a sort of magic talisman, so much so that Tiberius sends the officer to regain and destroy it, and at the same time to investigate the activities of the Christians. Needless to say, he is converted and, together with the girl he loves, dies a martyr's death. The film received more attention than it merited owing to its being the first full-scale Cinemascope release—and it should not be criticised for the technical drawbacks of an untried medium. In itself it is much the usual Bible epic stuff, adapted from a novel of extreme turgidity and religiosity by Lloyd C. Douglas. Rome is divided as sharply as usual: naughty, gaudy Emperors, simple, ungaudy Christians, and, in between, tormented but finally clear-eyed converts.

Somewhat later Christians are concerned in the Italian *Constantine the Great* (1960, *dir.* Lionello De Felice), but they are surrounded by much the same circumstances. The main facts of history are fairly closely adhered to, as far as the film goes, but the Eusebian version of Constantine's vision of the Cross in the sky forms the climax—though in actual fact Eusebius did not mention this story until twenty-five years later, a contemporary calls it a dream, and Constantine himself did not speak of it. The immense and lasting significance of his conversion is nowhere indicated and the whole question of the cause and completeness of the event is ignored. The film finishes thirteen years before his death—years of great activity and importance. Dull acting, a silly "story" and—of course—appalling dubbing, complete the ruin of what might have been a significant historical chronicle.

CRUSADES

First in the field again, Italy brought out *Jerusalem Liberated* from Cines in 1913, and *The Crusade of the Innocents* in the following year, based on a Mystery Play by Gabrielle D'Annunzio. The latter is described by a contemporary as an "original though not very satisfactory work."

Cecil B. DeMille is not at his best in *The Crusades* (1933), though it is one of his own favourites. The year 1187 was chosen as a focal point and seven Crusades were welded into one—"history condensed and dramatically rearranged," to use his own words. This in itself need not have proved unacceptable—a Crusadal distillation, as it were—but unfortunately the result is more like a large-scale pageant than a dramatic re-arrangement of history. "Authenticity of costuming" is not enough. The director discusses his intentions interestingly in his book and on the whole it must be admitted that, despite the film's faults, he has realised them well.

To compare *King Richard and the Crusaders* (1954, *dir.* David Butler) with the above is to show just how eminent DeMille is on his own ground. Supposed to deal with the Third Crusade and to be based on Scott's *The Talisman,* the film turns the whole concern into a conventional love triangle —Saladin falling in love with an English Lady on a pilgrimage and incurring the jealousy of her lover. Religion, even the tarnished faith used to excuse the actual Crusades, is almost non-existent, and good performances by George Sanders and Rex Harrison are unable to bring the film to life.

2. Christ in the Cinema

THE EARLIEST REPRESENTATIONS of Jesus on film were in a series of straightforward recordings of various Passion Plays. One of the first was made by two American theatrical producers, Marc Klaw and Abraham Erlanger, in Horitz, Bohemia. This was in 1897, and the following year a more elaborate rival was produced by R. G. Hollaman and A. G. Eaves—photographed on the roof of a New York building, with a script derived from a projected stage production of some years previously, which had failed to materialise. The length of the film was 2,100 feet—exceptionally long for the period—and a narrator took the place of captions. A full account of this film is given in Terry Ramsaye's *A Million and One Nights*. The Oberammergau Passion Play was photographed around the same time by a Mr. Hurd, Lumière's American representative, and this was followed in France by another rooftop version for the Musée Eden. Other French *Passions* include one by V. Jasset and Alice Guy (1906), in which Golgotha was reproduced at Fontainebleau and a gramophone was played to help the actors with their emotions—perhaps the earliest use of this artificial aid—and, possibly best known of all, one by Ferdinand Zecca, inspired by contemporary chromo-lithographs and some 2,000 feet in length. The date is variously given as 1903, 1905 and 1907—according to Georges Sadoul it was shot during the period 1902–5. It made use of panning shots, an innovation at the time. Despite some concern as to the reverence of showing Christ in person in the screen other hastily prepared *Passions* and *Lives* (often little more than a series of crude "living tableaux") proliferated, of which all traces have been lost. Several came from the Italian Cines company. Pathé produced a three-reel *Life of Christ* in 1908 which was in colour. It was later expanded to seven reels (1914) and later still further enlarged with a modern prologue (1921). France also produced *The Kiss of Judas* and *The Birth of Jesus* (in colour), both in 1909. The same year saw Edison's *Star of Bethlehem*. Other films of the birth of Christ followed—in one of which the Angel Gabriel appeared in full armour. Charles Kent played Christ and Julia Swayne Gordon played Mary Magdalene in Vitagraph's *Though Your Sins Be as Scarlet* in 1911. An Italian spectacle in four parts, *Satan: or the Drama of Humanity* came from Ambrosio in 1912, directed by Luigi Maggi. The second episode concerned the life of Christ.

Modern films of the period in which Christ appeared include Pathé's *Saved by Divine Providence*, where a vision of Jesus leads a mother to her lost son, *The Mysterious Stranger*, in which He restores a dead girl to life, and *The Carpenter*, in which, as a "Stranger in gray" He reconciles a family split by the Civil War—being represented, presumably, as having Southern sympathies. A primitive version of *Ben Hur* came from Kalem in 1908 (*dir.* Sidney Olcott), but I have been unable to discover whether it included the appearance of Christ or any symbol of His presence. An existing still shows Jesus being mocked and crowned with thorns in an Italian film, *The Pilgrim* (1912, *dir.* Caserini)—this should not be confused with another of the same title a few years later, which told the story of St. Francis.

The first major Life, still shown today, also appeared in 1912. This is Sidney Olcott's famous *From the Manger to the Cross*. The scenarist, Gene Gauntier, reputedly conceived the idea while in delirium following an attack of sunstroke, and prepared the script against the wishes of the Company, Kalem. In the event, it was a great and lasting success. The film was shot in Egypt and Palestine and Miss Gauntier herself played the Virgin Mary. R. Henderson Bland was both dignified and

The first major "Life of Christ": FROM THE MANGER TO THE CROSS.

moving as Christ (he afterwards became a military hero in the First World War). As the title implies, the life of Jesus is only shown from His babyhood—four successive children portraying His growth—to His death on the Cross. Some fears had been experienced as to its reception among religious bodies, but a special showing soon removed these doubts, the Bishop of London declaring it to be superior to the Oberammergau Passion. The film has of course some crudities of technique to modern eyes, particularly in the larger crowd scenes—others, on the contrary, are the more effective for their simplicity, for instance the Crucifixion. The Way to the Cross was shot on the actual Via Dolorosa in Jerusalem. In 1938, at Henderson Bland's suggestion, the Rev. Brian Hession added a soundtrack and a few close-ups for a reissue. Despite the great success of the film, Gene Gauntier and Sidney Olcott were both forced to leave Kalem as a result of their insistence on making it.

About this time an organisation known as the "Bonne Cinéma," set up in Paris by the Augustinian fathers for the promulgation of good film, was starting to use churches as a normal place for projecting them. Pope Pius X at first said that during Lent motion pictures should not be shown in churches, then, in a Decree at the end of 1912, instructed that "even religious films were not to be projected in churches, in order that the sacred character of the buildings should be safeguarded."

The figure of Christ appears briefly in Thomas Ince's pacifist film *Civilization* (1915, *dir.* Raymond B. West), in which the hero refuses to fire a torpedo against a passenger ship (foreshadowing the Lusitania) and is imprisoned for advocating peace. The Spirit of Christ (impersonated by George Fisher) enters into his body to work for the abolition of war. It is never divulged what the war is about nor who are the protagonists—the theme being that *all* war is evil. The treatment was naïve and over-simplified, however, and the announcement in May 1917 that the film had been "rearranged with new titles, inserts of the American flag and of Wilson's great message to Congress," (i.e. on the U.S. entry into the First World War), needs no elaboration as a comment on the sincerity of some film-makers. Whether Ince was agreeable to the mutilation of his picture is not stated.

The Judean story of Griffith's *Intolerance* concerns the teaching and death of Jesus (played by Howard Gaye as "The Nazarene") and shows several incidents such as the marriage

36

at Cana, the woman taken in adultery, the Way to the Cross and the Crucifixion. Gaye is a grave and gentle Christ, and the scenes on the road to Golgotha in particular convey something of the sense of high tragedy. Around the same period the Italian Cines company issued a large-scale *Christus* (dir. Giulio Antomoro) with Giovanni Pasquali as Christ. Described as a "poem by Fausto Salvatori," it was filmed in Egypt and designed after famous paintings. It was very successful and was revived every Easter for years in various countries.

In the first of the four parts of Carl Dreyer's *Leaves from Satan's Book* (1922) the Devil disguises himself as the Pharisee who leads Judas to betray Christ, a curious example of the transference of guilt. The whole film has a similar form to Griffith's *Intolerance,* but with betrayal as the recurring theme. Halvard Hoff appears as Jesus. Robert Wiene's *I.N.R.I.* (1923) is about a sentenced murderer who is told the life of Christ by the chaplain, the recounted scenes being enacted in the form of a Passion Play. The murderer, who has shot an official to free his country from oppression, repents. Siegfried Kracauer, in his well-known book on the foreshadowing of Nazism in the German films of the period, *From Caligari to Hitler,* sees in this story a comment on the political significance of religious conversion. Gregor Chmara (later one of the numerous actors to play Rasputin), is Christ, Henny Porten the Virgin Mary and Asta Nielsen Mary Magdalene. In 1934 the film was reissued as *Crown of Thorns.*

The hero of *Ben Hur* is a contemporary of Jesus Christ, and in Lew Wallace's book their lives run parallel courses which incidentally cross on a few occasions, real and fictitious events being mingled on the whole with success. In the famous 1926 version (dir. Fred Niblo) His presence is generally indicated by a hand, or both hands. His feet, or a headless trunk. Although not the *cliché* it was later to become, this sort of jigsaw coyness was even then irritating, particularly as the picture proceeds. In addition, the hand seen was ludicrously unlikely, being white, slim, with delicate tapering fingers, suggesting an effete fop or a woman living in idle luxury. In the original print all the "Christ" scenes were in colour, thus further destroying the sense of reality. The Last Supper was shown as a replica of Da Vinci's famous but of course deliberately anachronistic painting. At the end of the film, superimposed on the scene of the Crucifixion (with the two lovers prominent in the foreground) are the words: "He died—but Love goes on for ever." Against this sort of thing must be set the brief but exquisite appearance of Betty Bronson (lovely and insufficiently appreciated actress of the silent screen) as the Virgin Mary.

In 1927 came Cecil B. DeMille's *The King of Kings*, the most famous, most discussed and costliest religious film made up to that point. The action starts when Jesus is already fully grown and preaching—His childhood and youth being omitted. The first half deals with selected events occurring during His ministry, among them the casting out of the seven deadly sins from Mary Magdalene, the raising of Lazarus, the driving of the money-changers from the Temple (after which the temptation by Satan is inserted) and the teaching of the Lord's Prayer. The second half concentrates on the Passion: the betrayal by Judas, the trial, the Way to the Cross, death and Resurrection—followed almost immediately—by a concentration of the recorded events—by the Ascension. Originally fifteen reels long, the film was later cut to eleven by the deletion of a number of scenes such as the calling of the disciples, and the discussion over the payment of tribute money. Throughout the filming a Jesuit, a priest from the Federal Council of Churches, and another member of the clergy were present to give advice. In order to avoid offending Jewish susceptibilities (an attempt which did not succeed) Caiaphas, rather than Judas, was made responsible for Christ's death. Extraordinary steps were taken (and publicised) to ensure a proper attitude of reverence. H. B. Warner (Christ) was spoken to by no-one save the director when in costume, veiled and transported in a closed car when necessary, and on location given his meals in solitude. Prayers were said at the scene of the Crucifixion (which was filmed on Christmas Eve), Mass was celebrated every morning on location. The first day of shooting started with the uttering of prayers by representatives of Protestant, Catholic, Jewish, Buddhist and Moslem faiths.

The film itself shows DeMille at his best, and at his worst. It begins appallingly with a Mary Magdalene living in conditions of unbelievable splendour, bejewelled and be-silked, surrounded by marble palaces and baths, leopards, zebras, revellers and slaves. This sequence was originally in colour. Judas, it seems, is her lover but has been playing truant a good deal lately. Off she goes in a tantrum to see "this carpenter" who has lured him away. Then, of course, she falls for the "carpenter"—and we are prepared for anything. To start with, as R. P. Messel points out, the fact that Mary Magdalene made so sudden a change from harlotry to virtue suggests that her previous career was not exactly successful, and the fact that she came in touch with Jesus at all indicates that she was not a great courtesan of the Thais variety. The gospel story is reduced to the level of a sex triangle, with even nastier undertones, and the future is filled with foreboding. Astonishingly, from then on DeMille—as if he had expelled it from his system—turns his back on such extravagances and produces a film of rare restraint and dignity, which, within its convention, is unsurpassed today. It is, of course, "pretty-picture-book," but regarded on this level there is much to commend. H. B. Warner

gives a superb performance, wholly inspired and inspiring—
in appearance half-way between the silken-haired, fragile,
feminine figure of Victorian colour supplements and the
tougher, more realistic portrayals of later years. The first sight
of Christ's face is wonderfully contrived. A young blind girl
is among a crowd outside a fisherman's hut listening to a boy's
story of a man inside who has cured his lameness. The girl
is taken into the hut. All goes dark as we are placed behind
her sightless eyes. Gradually, from all corners of the screen,
rays of light begin to radiate, growing ever brighter and more
concentrated until—at first in a haze, then clearly—she sees the
gentle face of her Healer smiling down at her. In forty years
the scene has lost none of its power, and it is easy to believe
the American minister who told Warner some time later: "I
saw you in *The King of Kings* when I was a child and now,
every time I speak of Jesus, it is your face I see."

The disciples are unusually well differentiated, characters
with their own entity rather than a handful of supporters with
one or two standing out, as in other versions. Ernest Torrence
is a splendidly impetuous, lovable Peter and Joseph Schild-
kraut's Judas, if somewhat theatrical, is the most arresting yet
seen. Alan Brooks is Satan in a highly original handling of
the temptation scene.

The question, which has often been raised, as to how much
all the fuss over good conduct during the filming, the silence,
the prayers, etc., was ballyhoo is irrelevant. What is important
is the effect the finished film had on *contemporary* audiences.
It met with considerable criticism on such counts at the time,
as did the carefully contrived cathedral atmosphere in the
various cinemas—organ-playing, hymn-singing, staged "reli-

"Every time I speak of Jesus, it is your face I see":
H. B. Warner as THE KING OF KINGS (1927)

gious" preludes. But when all this is set aside, many who saw those first performances carried away something deeper than the memory of just another DeMille epic—and there must be more than a few who would echo the words of the minister quoted above.

No film of note on Christ followed *The King of Kings* until Julien Duvivier's *Golgotha*, eight years later, the first to be made in sound, with music by Jacques Ibert. It covers, as the title implies, only the events of Holy Week. Robert le Vigan is the Christ and, an interesting piece of casting, Jean Gabin is Pontius Pilate. At some time during this period the Ober-ammergau Passion was filmed silent, with spoken prologue and a musical score. The 1935 *Last Days of Pompeii* (*dir*. Ernest B. Schoedsack) is not based on Lytton's novel, but deals with an unfortunate young blacksmith who becomes a gladi-ator, a slave dealer and then overseer of the Pompeiian arena. His son is healed by "The Teacher," and the father is con-verted, but denies Him before Calvary. Eventually he loses his life trying to save others during the Vesuvius eruption, whereupon the Teacher appears in a shadowy form and utters the words beginning "Greater love hath no man . . . " The film's main interest lies in Basil Rathbone's portrayal of Pilate.

A Christ figure in modern setting appears in *Strange Cargo* (1940, *dir*. Frank Borzage), an odd little film starring Clark Gable. On arrival back in camp from their day's labour, a party of prisoners on Devil's Island is found to include an extra man, played by Ian Hunter, who seems to have super-normal knowledge of the other convicts' lives, and seeks to develop their "better natures." Gable, as a scoffing unbeliever, hurls the Stranger into the sea during a furious quarrel. The Stranger clutches a wooden plank, assuming a crucifixion-like posture. Gable realises the Stranger is, in fact, of divine origin, and is converted to belief in God. The Stranger disappears into the darkness. A minor film, but not without a certain atmosphere.

Luis Alcoriza played the part of Jesus of Nazareth in a Mexican film entitled *Maria Magdalena* (dir. Miguel Torres) in 1946, and received praise for an impressive performance in a deeply felt and fairly successful production. As mentioned in the previous chapter, events from the life of Christ are shown as tableaux during a sermon by St. Peter in the 1951 *Quo Vadis.* In the following year Robert S. Flaherty made the *St. Matthew Passion,* based on the choral work by J. S. Bach, which is used to accompany well-known paintings from different countries depicting the events of Passion Week.

The Crucifixion scene in *The Robe* (1953) is one of the more successful in that generally mediocre offering. The Cinemascope screen is used to some effect, even attaining a hint of tragic grandeur. Christ's words from the Cross are heard (spoken by Cameron Mitchell) while we are shown the agonised upwards-gazing face of a Greek slave (Victor Mature). The scene has been accused of vulgarity, particularly as regards the blood dropping on to Mature's hand—but a death by crucifying *is* a matter of blood and agony, and at least the attempt is made to avoid from the calm, painless repose so often depicted. Also shown is the Entry into Jerusalem.

A short of great beauty is Lotte Reiniger's animated film of the visit of the Kings to the manger—*The Star of Bethlehem* (1956). It is her first colour film, showing the familiar black silhouetted figures against delicately tinted backgrounds. The version shown in England was apparently crudely cut, thus destroying the film's continuity and rhythm.

Jules Dassin's *He Who Must Die* (1957) links the gospel story with the plight of the Greeks persecuted by the Turks in Crete during 1921. The cast of a village Passion Play begin to adapt their roles to their real-life situation. It is a large-

BEN HUR (1959) . . . .

scale, deeply sincere work. Pierre Vaneck plays the actor portraying Christ. A strange little Italo-American film of 1959 is *Desert Desperadoes* (alternatively titled *Flight into Egypt*), which uses the flight of Mary and Joseph with the Child as a background for an altogether different story. The baby Jesus is not actually shown.

The same year saw the appearance of the most recent and ambitious *Ben Hur* (*dir.* William Wyler). Shot in Italy, the film is visually highly exciting, even if the chariot-race seems less breathtaking than (in memory) that in the old silent

.... *KING OF KINGS (1961)*

version. Christ is pictured more boldly (by Claude Heater) than in the irritating hand-and-foot business of the 1926 production, but even so He is a vague and unsatisfying figure. The portrayal of Pontius Pilate as an effeminate fop is a cheap and unjustified gimmick.

With *The Big Fisherman* (1959, *dir*. Frank Borzage) we are back to hands and robe-hems—plus quite an impressive voice "off"—and also to Lloyd C. Douglas, author of *The Robe*. What could have been a significant and moving story of the great and human Peter is trivialised, and even the recorded events of the gospels are distorted. The film ends before the Crucifixion and, as a critic remarks, it seems unlikely that this climax would ever have occurred, as Christ is shown as not having an enemy in the world, all the Scribes, Pharisees and priests being completely in favour of Him.

Another large—in both senses—disappointment is the 1961 *King of Kings*, though it would seem that the blame should not be laid wholly at the feet of the director, Nicholas Ray, according to whom the film was "atrociously edited" after it had left his hands. The treatment of the story as a sort of anti-Nazi underground movement, with Barabbas and Judas working together(!) to destroy Roman oppression and with Jesus being caught up in the general political upheaval, might have been an interesting if not very valid interpretation. The lack of emphasis on Christ's divinity, the omission of the miracles, the interpolated scenes such as Christ's visit to John the Baptist in his cell, these also might have been acceptable. The film is weakened, however, by other misjudgements such as the introduction of irrelevant battle spectacles, the coloured supplement *décor,* and above all the casting of Christ (Jeffrey Hunter). The film was reputedly known to the trade as "I was a teenage Jesus." One piece of casting, however, deserves all praise—at last we are given a Salome somewhere near the age she should be.

The incredible story of Robert Frank's *The Sin of Jesus* (1961) concerns a woman-servant in a hotel who is six months pregnant by the janitor. She has already had twins by him, and he now deserts her. She thereupon appeals to Jesus, who presents her with an angel-husband for four years, but stipulates that he must take off his wings before getting into bed. The woman gets drunk, and, heavy with child, rolls on top of the angel and kills him. Jesus is furious with her for smothering his angel, bawling at her with such Christ-like

*KING OF KINGS (1961):
Robert Ryan as John the
Baptist, Brigid Bazlen
as a credible Salome.*

expressions as "You filthy scum!" Later He asks her forgiveness, which she refuses. It is just conceivable that this farrago is intended to make some obscure comment after the manner of television "satire"—the question is how far offensiveness and sheer silliness can go before losing claim to even that dubious result.

In *Barabbas* (1962), discussed in the previous chapter, the appearance of Jesus is contrived rather in the same way as in DeMille's *King of Kings*: on emerging from his dark prison, Barabbas sees Jesus enveloped and irradiated in a blinding glow of sunlight. Several events of Holy Week are shown, but a view of Christ's face in full is avoided.

A short film of 1964, *Rembrandt's Christ*, shows over a hundred of the artist's drawings of the life of Jesus, so arranged as to tell the story without words. As a piece of film-making the result has been criticised, but is probably of interest to anyone anxious to study the subject indicated in its title.

It is difficult to understand the widespread—but by no means universal—condemnation of George Stevens's *The Greatest Story Ever Told* (1965). Admittedly, the film is overlong, apt to become embedded in a cotton wool "piety," crammed with big names so that it becomes a sort of 'spot-the-star-before-he's-gone' game. Admittedly, too, the attempt to exonerate Judas—for which there is a definite case—is done with insufficient conviction to avoid weakening and, oddly, trivialising both the Betrayal and that which ensues. The parables are omitted, Judas's method of suicide is changed, the script is not free from the usual ill-chosen lines (how fortunate DeMille was in making *his* Life during the silent days!), and other incongruities occur. But individual sequences, such as the raising of Lazarus (praised even by the grudgers) and the Crucifixion are magnificent, Telly Savalas and Claude Rains are convincing as Pilate and Herod the Great respectively, and, above all, Max von Sydow is a strong, virile, compassionate and even at times a humorous Christ. Edward Connor describes him as the best since H. B. Warner—it is arguable that he even surpasses the earlier performance. Warner, for all the beauty, tenderness and dignity of his portrayal, or perhaps because of these very virtues, never quite convinced as the Son of Man as well as the Son of God. Warner was the "gentle Jesus" of the child's bedside as well as the Teacher, the Healer, the Reformer, the Man

*Max von Sydow as Christ in THE GREATEST STORY
EVER TOLD*

of unquenchable will and inner determination. Von Sydow
satisfies one on all these points, but in addition is also the
trudger from place to place through the hot dusty countryside,
the craftsman's son. The physical strength to undergo the
strains imposed on Christ is evident in von Sydow—with
Warner one occasionally has doubts in this one respect. The
film was a costly failure, and it is a pity that, because of

adverse criticism, many people may not now have the chance of seeing von Sydow's portrayal.

In 1965 Empire Films released *The Redeemer* in America. I have come across no mention of its having been shown in England. It is a compilation of a number of motion pictures, usually two-reelers, produced under the inspiration of Fr. Christopher Peyton, who organised what was called a "Rosary Crusade" and secured the assistance of a number of players such as Loretta Young and Bing Crosby. The films were built, more or less loosely, round the fifteen mysteries of the Rosary. Fr. Peyton secured the services of actors in various countries in which he preached his crusade. The Spanish actor Luis Alvarez, plays Christ (seen mainly from the back), and the words are spoken by Macdonald Carey.

Pier Paolo Pasolini's *Gospel According to St. Matthew* made an enormous impact when it appeared in 1964. A Communist, the director has not given, as might have been expected, an ideological interpretation of the life of Christ, but has adhered closely, one might almost say coldly, to both the spirit and the facts of this one Gospel. Only at the Crucifixion is emotion, in the person of the Virgin Mary, allowed free rein, and the effect (at a first viewing) is shattering. Shot in Southern Italy on a very tight budget, the photography, full of glaring chalky whites and dusty greys, strikingly reproduces the "feel" of the Palestinian background. The music, ranging boldly from Bach to a Congolese Mass, is strongly effective, the sometimes harsh recording matching the austere naturalistic treatment of the whole. Pasolini's use of huge facial close-ups often reminds one of Dreyer's *Passion of Joan of Arc*, particularly in the cases of the minor parts—Pharisees and priests in towering, arrogant head-dresses, the two Herods, soldiers, and the young man with great possessions. Others call to mind early Italian paintings—notably the beautiful Botticelli-like angel, almost wholly humanised—yet far more convincingly other-worldly than the conventional winged and chubby figures. (Where, incidentally, are the tremendous muscles necessary to work those monstrous wings?) Numerous scenes remain unforgettable: the death of Herod, shuddering to extinction on a stone slab while the priests sit around the wall waiting in solemn, cold, relentless patience for the end; Jesus as a tiny boy running and stumbling to Joseph's outstretched hands; the radiant, unglamorous young Mary, both welcoming and resigned to the role that awaits her; the dance of the blank-eyed, virginal, sacrificial Salome, conveying more of the corruption surrounding her than the lustiest of Technicolor orgies; Christ on trial, glimpsed from afar through a camera that

Enrique Irazoqui as Christ:
THE GOSPEL ACCORDING TO ST. MATTHEW

dodges and peeps over the shoulders of the watchers and guards in the courtyard; above all, Marcello Morante's wonderful Joseph, obeying with grave, gentle dignity and love the commands he half comprehends.

All these, and other scenes, are reinforced by subsequent viewings. The film's impact as a whole, however, is unexpectedly weaker when seen a second time. In particular the agony of the watchers at the Crucifixion, almost unbearably moving on the first occasion, seems much too protracted, despite Susanna Pasolini's great performance as the grown Mary —though she is, surely, much too old? Christ, played by Enrique Irazoqui, a young Spanish student, and dubbed quite creditably into Italian, becomes a strangely unlovable figure; almost, in fact, a bit of a bore at times, despite much fire, authority and passion. Surely, one feels, despite the stern duties before Him, despite the necessity for grave commitment, and knowledge of tragedy to come, surely Christ *smiled* more often than this? The literal, non-commenting treatment of the text strengthens the great drama in many instances—in others it weakens it, notably in regard to the miracles. The "healing of the leper" by a straight cut from the man's made-up mutilated face to his unmade-up perfect one, accompanied by a sharp burst of heavenly music, resembles nothing so much as a cheap horror film effect worked backwards. It reduces a miracle to a rudimentary camera trick. The walking on the water, with Christ standing, feet awash, on a submerged raft, looks merely what it is, and the "five thousand" waiting to be fed have shrunk to a mere handful. If the budget did not allow

Right, THE GOSPEL ACCORDING TO ST. MATTHEW:
Top, Enrique Irazoqui as Christ
Below, Marcello Morante unforgettably playing
Joseph, with Margherita Caruso as the Virgin Mary

an actual 5,000 extras, it should surely have been possible to suggest their presence. The apostles are never easily identifiable (as they were in DeMille's film) and a strange quirk of casting has resulted in Judas and Peter resembling each other so that on more than one occasion they are apt to be confused. The episode of Peter's denial, one of the most moving in the entire Bible, is handled so casually as to lose most of its power. Peter, after all, "began to curse and to swear, saying 'I know not the man.'" Here the disowning is so offhand that the ensuing bitter remorse is also weakened. All in all, however, the admirable qualities of this often beautiful and memorable film outweigh any shortcomings—and always there is Morante's brief but unforgettable playing as Joseph.

It is interesting to note that Pasolini dedicated his film to Pope John XXIII. The director was in Florence, and was held up in an enormous traffic jam caused by the Pope's visit. He booked a room in a hotel for the time involved, found a copy of the New Testament, and spent the time reading St. Matthew's Gospel. It was thus that he decided to make his film, and decided also to dedicate it to the Pope.

A project for the life of Christ, *The Divine Tragedy*, to be directed by Abel Gance, was under way in 1949, but unfortunately had to be dropped for lack of money. It was to have been shot in Egypt and Switzerland, with a non-professional cast, Christ being played by a French mathematics professor.

An even greater loss has been caused by the death of Carl Dreyer. For twenty years he had been preparing for a film on the life of Christ, always to be held up by lack of finance. A grant by the Danish Government's Film Fund had made the production a possibility. The film was to have started with Jesus as a grown man, kept closely to the Gospel stories, and been treated in a manner "neither naturalistic nor documentary, but simplified like a modern woodcut."

3. Priests, Ministers and the Church

ONE OF THE EARLIEST of many studies of the struggles between the religious conscience and the world appeared in 1915—a British adaptation of the famous Hall Caine novel *The Christian,* directed by G. L. Tucker. The same year also saw the first portrayal of Richelieu, in a version, also British, of Stanley Weyman's *Under the Red Robe* (*dir.* Wilfred Noy), with Owen Roughwood as the Cardinal, and Dorothy Drake. By 1923 both had crossed the Atlantic. *The Christian* in that year was directed by Maurice Tourneur, filmed partly on location in the Isle of Man, and starring Richard Dix (demonstrating, as he did in the modern story of DeMille's *Ten Commandments,* that he is one of the comparatively few actors who can be "good" without also being either boring or smug). Robert B. Mantell is a somewhat beefy Richelieu in *Under the Red Robe* (also 1923, *dir.* Alan Crosland), with the beautiful Alma Rubens and a villainous William Powell.

A still of 1917 shows Stuart Holmes (later a famous silent heavy) emoting violently in *The Scarlet Letter,* with Mary Martin as Hester clinging to one arm and a coy little girl named Kittens Reichert sheltering beneath the other. The Pastor's moustaches look strangely out of place. Sidney Olcott and Gene Gauntier, the team responsible for *From the Manger to the Cross,* were director and scenarist. But Hawthorne's classic had to await Lillian Gish and Lars Hanson before coming into its own.

Nigel de Brulier's Dom Claude, though a minor part, stands out in the 1923 *Hunchback of Notre Dame* (*dir.* Wallace Worsley), the deep-eyed ascetic features of this fine character actor bringing distinction to one more of his "committed" roles. Edmund Lowe appeared as a somewhat self-consciously tormented priest in Channing Pollock's *The Fool* in 1924, and

Milton Sills played yet another opposite Nazimova in *The Madonna of the Streets* in 1925. Sills was an actor of considerable presence and, like Richard Dix, was able to preach without preachiness, and to leaven a doughy role with a touch of humour. His performance as the priest endeavouring to "do the right thing" by both body and soul lifted a hoary melodrama into a compassionate study of human conflict.

One of the most famous of all silent films, *The Scarlet Letter* (*dir.* Victor Sjöström) was produced in 1926—beautifully photographed, directed and played. Though Lillian Gish may not be quite the doughty Hester Prynne of Hawthorne's novel, she comes much closer to it, particularly as the climax of the film approaches, than some critics have allowed. She entirely convinces us of her ability to persuade the pastor to keep quiet about the fact that he is the father of her child because of the importance of his work to the little community, and her gradual transition from the light-hearted girl to the ferocious defender of her child and her secret is completely credible and often very moving. It is throughout, as Edward Wagenknecht says, "a profound and beautiful study." Lars Hanson powerfully supports her and the final scene, when, tortured by conscience when Hester's lost husband returns, the pastor confesses in public and dies in her arms, is as affecting today, in a scratched and jerky print, as when the film made its noteworthy first appearance. The 1934 re-make (*dir.* Robert C. Vignola) does not stand comparison. Hardie Albright is just a pleasant young American dressed up in costume, and Colleen Moore, most charming of comediennes, cannot compare in more tragic matters with Lillian Gish.

Brief mention should be made of the silent *Bridge of San Luis Rey* (*dir.* Charles Brabin) on account of Henry B. Walthall's fine acting in the small part of Father Juniper, trying to justify to his congregation the Almighty purpose behind the apparently arbitrary deaths of the victims of the broken bridge. It is a beautiful film altogether, with another outstanding character performance from Emily Fitzroy.

The last silent film to be mentioned is an oddity—Germaine Dulac's *The Seashell and the Clergyman*, an *avant-garde* surrealist story of a young clergyman's frustrated sexuality, in which he is seen pursuing a woman in white through a series of dreamlike events, and is perpetually thwarted. The film's approach is ambiguous, some seeing it as a dream and others as a study in psycho-analysis. Antonin Artaud, the author (who stated himself that it is *not* a dream), plays the clergyman. Shortly afterwards he appeared as the young priest in Dreyer's *Passion of Joan of Arc,* a performance of the utmost power and beauty.

Spencer Tracy launched his "priest among men" in *San Francisco* (1936), following it up as a "priest among boys" in *Boys' Town* in 1938. W. S. Van Dyke directed the former, Norman Taurog the latter. Tracy's Father Flanagan of *Boys' Town* and its less successful *Men of Boys' Town* (1941) is founded on a real character. The warmth, sincerity and humour of Tracy's performance keep the films almost free of the mawkishness which threatens on such occasions—a threat which comes to pass in Pat O'Brien's attempt to convert the Dead End Kids in *Angels with Dirty Faces* (1938, *dir.* Michael Curtiz), a film as embarrassing as its title implies, despite O'Brien's credible and likeable priest. The wholly contrived ending, with James Cagney pretending to go to his death a coward in order to convert the surviving Kids, ranks high among uncomfortable moments in the cinema. Several years later, as another parson (though notably similar to the former) Pat O'Brien was given much better material in *Fighting Father Dunne* (1947, *dir.* Ted Tetzlaff), and the result was a satisfying, if conventional portrayal of a man and a priest. His Fight is to found a home for boys, in the course of which he obtains newsrounds for them. The treatment is unsentimental, and does not pretend that to be underprivileged is necessarily to be a saint.

An inexplicably neglected film of 1940 was Roy Boulting's *Pastor Hall*, adapted from a play by Ernst Toller which is based on the arrest and imprisonment by the Nazis of Pastor Niemuller. In the film, the Pastor escapes from the camp in which he has been detained, but instead of seeking safety in flight to America he preaches a sermon denouncing the Nazi creed from his pulpit, then walks down the aisle to the waiting S.S. men outside, and to death. Wilfrid Lawson gives a masterly performance and the film certainly deserves revival—if it still exists.

Gustaf Molander's *The Word* (1943) tells the story of an old man (Victor Sjöström) whose son, wishing to enter the church, worries himself half mad over religious doubts, then restores his dead sister-in-law to life by an outburst of fanatical faith. It is adapted from a play by Kaj Munk. Carl Dreyer, who had been anxious to make a film from it ever since its first production in 1932, directed a new adaptation in 1954. This second version was, as might be expected, conceived on more mystical lines than the first, and is notable for the formal beauty of many of its settings. The author was murdered by the Nazis shortly after the appearance of the Molander film.

1944 saw the first of Bing Crosby's crooning clergymen in *Going My Way* (*dir.* Leo McCarey), a glutinous mixture of sentimentality and saccharine in which Bing cheerfully proceeds to reorganise a church and converting young vandals into choristers. A "funny-irascible" old priest played by Barry Fitzgerald increases rather than lessens the slushy falseness of the whole affair, which leaves a nastier taste in the mouth than the worst Biblical blockbuster excesses—a taste made even harder to tolerate by the next in line from the same confectioners—*The Bells of St. Mary* (or St. Mary's, as preferred), in 1946, which has in addition Miss Ingrid Bergman and a bevy of singing nuns. As a contemporary critic pithily remarks, this is altogether "too much of a good Bing."

Aldo Fabrizi's Father Don Pietro, in *Open City* (1945, *dir.* Roberto Rossellini), who helps the Italian underground Resistance against the Nazis and goes to his death rather than betray his comrades, is a powerful figure. Apart from a few moments of sensationalism, such as the torture scene, the fire and drive of *Open City* make it a harrowing but inspiring experience to watch, with Fabrizi's priest as its formidable symbol.

An American film of the same year, *The Keys of the Kingdom* (*dir.* John M. Stahl) is a much slighter affair, but Gregory Peck's performance as the priest who, as a boy, sees his father killed because he is a Roman Catholic, and later himself forms a mission in China, has all the quiet integrity and sincerity of this actor at his best. He manages to create an unremarkable, ordinary, decent man who is not at the same time a dull figure: the result makes an unassuming and quite memorable film.

Symphonie Pastorale (1946, *dir.* Jean Delannoy) brings us another fundamentally good man, but one who sins through self-deception. There is in this moving French film a sense of Nemesis, of the flaw within the hero, which is found in the tragedy of the ancient Greeks. Pierre Blanchard plays the part of a pastor who in pity brings a blind child into his house and, as she grows up, falls in love with her, without realising it. His wife resents the girl's presence. His son also falls in love with the girl, whose sight is at length restored, but is forbidden by the Pastor to marry her. Eventually understanding the truth, the girl drowns herself. The plot, which in so compressed a synopsis sounds melodramatic (though no more so than that of many a Greek tragedy), is lifted out of the commonplace by Blanchard's finely sensitive if somewhat theatrical performance. Michèle Morgan plays the girl with a sort of fragile tenderness, and the film is most beautifully photographed—the pale purity of the snow-covered landscapes offering a calm and ironical contrast to the tormented human being for whom they form a background.

Monsieur Vincent (*dir.* Maurice Cloche), the "story" of St. Vincent de Paul, was released in 1947. The astonishing success of this film can only have been due to its fulfilling some barely realised emotional need of its period—an escapist delight to mystic idealism, perhaps, after the filth and misery of a long war and the inevitable disillusionment of "victory." In actual fact the film in itself is mediocre and pretty stodgy. It consists of a series of episodes with long intervening gaps (and St. Vincent's make-up appropriately ageing between each one), none of which form any coherent structure. It is historically inaccurate, both in some of its details (e.g. St. Vincent's death) and, more unfortunately, in its portrayal of the leading character who—though born the son of a peasant farmer, in time became an accomplished, cultured and intellectual man of his time and his world. A mere list of his posts and activities fills several lines of print, whereas the film deals only with his establishment of Saint Lazare and the Foundlings Hospital. There are, admittedly, a number of effective sequences—the galleys, the inaccurate death scene, in particular the scenes in the plague-stricken town, where the stench and filth and degradation are conveyed with sickening realism. But the parts do not add up to a consistent whole, although Pierre Fresnay makes the most of what he is given, and enables us to feel something of the burning sincerity of the great reformer

Right, MONSIEUR VINCENT:
Pierre Fresnay as
"the great reformer and lover of the poor"

and lover of the poor. The dialogue is literate, but dull: the photography ranges from the beautiful to the average. Even writers of the standing of Jean Bernard Luc and Jean Anouilh, however, have been unable to handle the mass of material which comprises the life of this astonishing man, and we are left with the conventional instead of the extraordinary. The furore it caused at the time of its London run inspired the magazine *Sequence* to a cartoon showing a long queue—choir-boys, nuns, clerics of every conceivable denomination and garb —waiting patiently outside the Curzon cinema behind the 6s. seats barrier, while from a taxi, its door held open by an obsequious Cardinal, emerges the tip of a triple tiara. It is interesting to note, incidentally, that the money to make *Monsieur Vincent* was raised by the efforts of a group of inter-ested priests and laymen, who made appeals from parish to parish. Ordinary Catholic members made their small contri-butions from each parish organisation. The director was a Catholic, but Fresnay himself a Protestant who had long wanted to make the film.

In John Ford's *The Fugitive* (1947), Henry Fonda portrays an obscure village priest who refuses to be silenced or barred from his ministrations by a Latin-American *régime* determined to suppress his religion. Persuaded by a girl, whose illegitimate child he has baptized, to flee the country, he is brought back and dies—but the memory of his stand lives on. Though harshly criticised as a travesty of Graham Greene's novel *The Power and the Glory,* the film is unpretentious, and the Mexican at-mosphere and landscape are well caught.

The Edge of Doom (1949, *dir.* Mark Robson) concerns a young truck-driver who, depressed by lack of money, a sense of guilt over the death of his mother, and a confused resent-ment against the Roman Catholic Church as personified in his parish priest, kills the old man when he refuses to pay for his mother's funeral. A younger priest watches over the murderer until he confesses and repents. The original novel (the author of which was a Catholic) is said to have dealt with the motives of crime and repentance in some depth, but the film, perhaps inevitably, handles such matters more shallowly and the sad script, weightily well-intentioned, is made the more depressing by its lack of any wider significance than its own events.

The story of St. John Baptist Vianney, Curé d'Ars (Arles), is told in Marcel Blistène's *Heaven and Earth (Le Sorcier du Ciel)*. Living in the last century, he set himself to fight for spiritual values against the materialism and atheism which he regarded as overwhelming his countryside and his people. The fame of his simple wisdom and goodness spread abroad so that people from as far away as England journeyed to him for guidance and help. In the film he is seen fighting for the souls of those in his care against the powers of the devil, personified in his arch-enemy an atheistic blacksmith. In tackling the difficulty of presenting a mystic on the screen, the film is courageous if not wholly successful, and affords Georges Rollin the opportunity of a convincing and apparently a physically quite accurate portrayal.

Robert Bresson's *Diary of a Country Priest* (1950) is made from his own adaptation of Georges Bernanos's classic novel. The original is, as the title implies, in the form of a diary and Bresson, making periodic references to this journal, is able to penetrate and analyse in depth the doubts, torments, ill-health and solitude of the young Catholic priest who is its writer. He meets with apathy from the children and the poor of his parish, with resistance from the rich—the Count and Countess in the Château. His attempts to solve their personal problems and family feuds incur open hostility. His health is poor, he drinks too much, he is filled with self-doubt. He visits a doctor, and is told he is suffering from cancer. He goes to see a defrocked priest, formerly a companion, and, in the house where the man now lives with a mistress, the young Catholic dies. The intimacy with which we are brought into the lonely priest's life, the mere extent of our knowledge of him by the time the film closes, lifts this seemingly grim, uncompromising story—told by Bresson with a sort of austere beauty—from the depressing experience one might expect, to something purifying, almost exhilarating. The film is shot on location, with an extensive use of close-up, reminding one (as do parts of the *Gospel According to St. Matthew* in a different way) of Dreyer's *Joan of Arc*—though it appears that at the time Bresson had not seen the earlier film. Claude Laydu received high praise for his sensitive performance—Bresson's directorial methods apparently caused several *crises de nerfs* among his cast, resulting in at least one major outburst between himself and his young star.

Pierre Fresnay in *Dieu a Besoin des Hommes* (1951, *dir.* Jean Delannoy—in translation *Isle of Sinners!*) plays a fisherman, Thomas, who is also the verger of the church on an island in Brittany inhabited by fishermen and their families. The local priest, having had enough of his primitive living conditions, leaves, and Thomas is called on to take over his duties. What could have been an original study of the difficulties of what one might call a non-frocked priest, however, is put aside in favour of highly melodramatic goings-on among the villagers themselves—and the chances of ironical comment are not taken. The film loses its balance, which is a pity, because fine photography, Fresnay's playing, and above all an occasional odd but genuine feeling of the "fear of God" could, if more imaginatively utilised, have resulted in an unusual and striking work.

George Hoellering's production of T. S. Eliot's *Murder in the Cathedral* also appeared in 1951, with a special opening scene written in by the author showing Becket on trial before the King. Apart from this addition, and an extended speech for the Herald, the film is a more or less straightforward version of the play. It was made in St. John's Church, St. John's Wood, with Eliot himself (unseen) speaking the words of the Fourth Tempter. The part of Becket is taken by a non-professional, Father John Groser.

In *The First Legion* (1951, *dir.* Douglas Sirk) no fewer than six well-known Hollywood players, led by Charles Boyer, appear as priests. The story deals with a "miraculous" cure of an old priest in a small town and the pilgrimages which result. The place is swamped by people seeking cures; some die, others, including a young crippled girl, are healed by faith, until the Vatican, understandably, asks what is going on.

On the lighter side in the same year appeared the first of Fernandel's amusing, rather charming but quite trivial *Don Camillo* films—the first of a series of battles between the priest and the Communist mayor (Gino Cervi)—battles in which no-one gets hurt because agreement is all too improbably reached whenever anything really serious crops up. Fernandel's characterisation is very much the conventional, cosy Catholic priest of this type of comedy—but one has only to call to mind certain Hollywood productions to see the differences possible within that convention.

The Italian *Maddalena* (1954, *dir.* Augusto Genina) concerns a village priest, Don Vincenzo, who is plotted against by a dissolute farmer. The latter brings a prostitute from the nearest town to play the Madonna in a Good Friday procession and to induce the priest to think she is an innocent orphan. Later circumstances cause her to confess the truth to Don Vincenzo—that her illegitimate child had been burnt to death in just such another religious procession and she had vowed vengeance on the Madonna. Various other highly coloured events, including a declared "miracle" by Maddalena, lead to her being stoned to death by the villagers when they learn the truth. Gino Cervi, Don Camillo's opponent in the Fernandel series, is the priest in this odd mixture.

One or two other clerical studies during this period may be briefly listed. Pierre Fresnay turns up again, but unfrocked this time, in *The Renegade Priest* (*Le Défroqué*), directed by Léo Joannon. Montgomery Clift is a priest who is arrested for murder from which he cannot clear himself because to do so would be to give away a secret of the confessional, in Alfred Hitchcock's *I Confess*. The penitent, of course, is no other than the real murderer. The film, shot on location in Quebec, has its moments of Hitchcockian suspense, but as a study of the religious conscience it is superficial. Ralph Richardson plays a gentle parish vicar in George More O'Ferrall's film version of the stage play by Wynyard Brown, *The Holly and the Ivy*. Though obviously from the theatre, this story of the apparently "dear old vicar" from whom all family troubles must be kept—until one somewhat conveniently catastrophic Christmas they all come tumbling out and reveal the old man as much broader and tougher than people think—is neither as sentimental nor as facile as might be expected. The dialogue, in its solid style, is intelligent and taut; its characters believable and interesting; its significance wider than the four walls of the cosy English vicarage. The result is a good, if minor, film. Another in the same *genre* is *Lease of Life* (1954, *dir.* Charles Frend), featuring Robert Donat as a country vicar with only a year to live. By the end of it he has nicely settled his own, and other people's, affairs. Not so sugary as it sounds, the film has a warmth and gentle sadness which goes far to disarm criticism—as well as a sincere performance from the inescapably sympathetic Donat. Karl Malden's strident priest in the overpraised *On the Waterfront* (1954, *dir.* Elia Kazan) is one of those tough men of God appearing in certain American films, who one hopes it is correct to describe as rarely encountered outside the cinema. For collectors there are Mickey Rooney as a fighting parson in a religious Western, *The Twinkle in God's Eye* (1955, *dir*. George Blair) and Humphrey Bogart as a false priest who, having taken on a true one's identity to escape from a Chinese War Lord, arrives in a mission, is later exposed, but pardoned by the Bishop for his sacrilege because of his good works in the meantime! (*The Left Hand of God*, 1955, *dir*. Edward Dmytryk.)

Robert Hamer's *Father Brown* (1954) is notable for Alec Guinness's portrayal of G. K. Chesterton's priest-cum-detective —so full of charm and character that his total lack of physical resemblance to the original is easily accepted. The religious aspect of the stories as Chesterton wrote them, where Brown is out to succour the souls as much as to uncover the bodily misdeeds of the wrongdoers, is played down, but present in the film if carefully sought; and Guinness's quirky, amusing priest would be a pleasure to welcome to any pulpit. A much greater pleasure, one would imagine, than the *Man Called Peter* (1955, *dir*. Henry Koster) whose sermons must have made many a pew feel hard. The film, based on the true life story of Peter Marshall as written by his wife, might have been quite an inspiring account of the poor young Scotsman's rise to prominence in America as a pastor after becoming convinced that he had been saved from death by God's own hand. Once again, however, it is a case of sincerity proving unhappily dull —despite a reasonably strong performance by Richard Todd— and on the whole the forebodings aroused by the title are only too justified.

Far more interesting is Peter Glenville's production of *The Prisoner* in the same year, a film illuminated by Alec Guinness's committed and moving performance. Adapted from Bridget

Boland's play of the same name, it is essentially a study of the relationship between a priest accused of treason by a totalitarian government, and his examiner—the latter most sensitively played by Jack Hawkins. Eschewing physical torture (but not discomfort), the authorities endeavour to break the Cardinal's spirit and extort a confession by probing and undermining his mental and spiritual defences. The examiner uncovers the fact that the man became a priest not from any true sense of vocation but in order to escape from his lowly and undignified beginnings. By a trick, he also elicits a confession that he never loved his mother. Finally he reveals the Cardinal's weakness to be, not pride as might have been expected, but humility. The Cardinal confesses his treason publicly, is denied the ultimate boon of death, is set free and passes out from prison among the silent crowds who until then had venerated him. By the end of their long, strange association, however, the examiner himself has weakened and now, watching the Cardinal's departure from behind a barred window, awaits his own examination. The subtle interplay between the two men forms the core of the film. One wishes, indeed, that it could have been developed even further than it is, and grudges the time spent on exterior shots showing life in the city, and an irrelevant love affair. The claustrophobic atmosphere of the imprisonment and examinations is weakened by this opening out of the enclosed structure. It is interesting to note that, contrary to widely held belief, the film is not in fact based on the character and ordeal of Cardinal Mindzenty. Brigid Boland had written the play before the Cardinal's trial and treatment were known of. The play was already well on in rehearsal, with a black-robed Monsignor as the central character, when the producer, Peter Glenville, remarked how magnificent it would look if he were dressed in scarlet. There and then the author changed her character into a Cardinal.

With the end of the decade we are back with Bing Crosby clerically crooning in *Say One for Me* (*dir.* Frank Tashlin). In a very different category is Terence Young's *Serious Charge*, a small budget production of Philip King's play about a parson accused by a grudge-bearing Teddy Boy of indecent assault. The subject was a courageous one for its time, and although the film deals with the worldly duties rather than the spiritual conflicts of a churchman, it nevertheless casts an interesting light on the special vulnerability of a priest in matters of personal concern. It is also distinguished by Anthony Quayle's strong and sympathetic performance as the vicar.

According to Jean-Pierre Melville's own statement, his *Léon Morin, Priest* (1961) has for its theme the impossibility of conversion (to Catholicism) after a certain age. The period is that of the Nazi occupation, and the story concerns a young Communist widow who goes to confession for the purpose of telling her confessor—whoever he may be—just what she thinks of his religion. He, however, gives her back in argument as good as he receives, ending up by lending her books on the subject. Finding him to be both young and handsome, and being herself physically frustrated on account of the circumstances of the war, she is at first embarrassed at the developing relationship; but later, as the theological discussions continue, a genuine friendship springs up between them. Eventually, quite sincerely, she tells him that she has become a convert to his faith. When he doubts this, it dawns on her that in reality she is in love with him. The priest feels himself to a certain extent responsible for this turn of events, as he has all along been aware of the risks they have both been running. The resolution of the problem is handled with sympathy and integrity, even if it is really brought about by fate (in the form of the Liberation) than by the will of the characters themselves. The outward circumstances of occupation, war, under-

Jean-Paul Belmondo as LEON MORIN, PRIEST
(with Emmanuelle Riva)

ground movements, the uncertainty of living and of life itself, are discreetly kept before us, making the heightened emotionalism of the personal situation appear entirely natural. The perhaps surprising casting of Jean-Paul Belmondo is a total success. Whether playing with the widow's little girl, quietly countering each of her attempted arguments, or deliberately— but impersonally—encouraging her friendship to help them both in their joint loneliness, his Léon Morin is consistently believable and likeable as priest and man.

Spencer Tracy returns to the church in *The Devil at 4*

O'Clock (1961, *dir.* Mervyn LeRoy), appearing as a drunken but fundamentally "good" parson in a South Sea Island settlement. It seems we have been here before. On the island is a leper colony and a volcano. The melodrama is mediocre, and the eruption of the volcano—not unexpected—is perhaps its own comment on the proceedings.

A re-make of Graham Greene's *The Power and the Glory* (1961, *dir.* Marc Daniels) aroused little interest, even with the presence of Laurence Olivier as the drink-sodden priest. Potentially more exciting (despite its title) was *The Hoodlum Priest* (1961, *dir.* Irvin Kershner), founded on the true story of a Jesuit, Father Clark, who, in trying to help delinquents and convicts, becomes almost as much an outcast from society as the criminals themselves. According to Don Murray, who played the part as well as being associated in the production, the character of the priest was very watered down—with the result that he became little more than just another man-amongst-men-type parson.

Ingmar Bergman's *Winter Light* has been criticised as sterile —but sterility of the spiritual kind is its subject, and every cinematic and scenic device is employed to examine, dissect and comment on this aspect of the pastor's situation. We meet him first as he celebrates Holy Communion with his little group of parishioners—among whom is his mistress, who is a school-teacher, and a fisherman, Jonas. The fisherman comes afterwards to Tomas, the pastor, for comfort because of his obsessive fear of the atomic bomb, now in the hands of the Chinese. Tomas is unable to help him—on the contrary, he reveals to Jonas his own sense of hopelessness and loss. Later, Tomas is unable even to respond any longer to his mistress, refusing violently to marry her—unable to forget the memory of his wife. In his despair, the fisherman kills himself. This event breaks ever so slightly the cold crust in which Tomas is encased. As the chill twilight fades into a chiller darkness in his church, empty except for the teacher and the crippled sidesman, he prepares to conduct Evensong. While she waits, Märta says to herself: "If I could only lead him out of his emptiness, away from his lie-god. If we could dare to show each other tenderness. If we could believe in a truth—if we could believe . . . " *Winter Light* must be one of the coldest —physically coldest—films ever made. Outside: "a cold, dark wind, a grey half-light, a light but insistent snowfall" (Bergman's words in the printed script)—inside: an old, half-empty church, a vestry, a deserted schoolroom. Tomas is unwell—significantly, he has a painful throat. As Peter Cowie points out, his physical illness is used as an "outward and visible sign of an inward and spiritual ailment." He is anxious and withdrawn, alone since the death of his wife five years earlier, deserted now—so he feels—by God Himself. The tight enclosed structure of the film symbolises and reinforces the enclosed separation of its characters. As much as anything it is a study of failure in communication—ironically set against the Communion Service at its start.

The Cardinal (1963, *dir.* Otto Preminger) is an enormous film based on the novel by Henry Morton Robinson, and following the life of a young priest, Stephen Fermoyle, from his ordination in 1917 to his appointment as Cardinal in 1939. On the thread of this story is hung a variety of situations in which the Catholic has to decide on the attitude which his conscience will permit him to adopt. With such a wide spread of characters, settings and years (the cast list is immense, and scattered with Fathers, Monsignors, Cardinals and Sisters), it

Right, WINTER LIGHT:
Top, Gunnar Björnstrand as the pastor
with Max von Sydow as the fisherman, Jonas
Below, the pastor with Märta (Ingrid Thulin)

is obvious that the various problems discussed, which range from intermarriage to Nazi infiltration, cannot be explored very deeply. However, on its own level as a 70 mm "epic" taken from a best-seller, it passes the time—175 minutes' worth.

In 1964 Richard Burton appeared as Becket in the film of Anouilh's play of that name, and also as the Rev. Laurence Shannon in Tennessee Williams's *The Night of the Iguana* (*dir.* John Huston)—who has been turned from his episcopal church because of a scandal concerning a young girl, and has become guide to a party of women teachers on a Mexican tour. The mood is comedy, even farce, but some reality of treatment is given to yet another frustrated clergyman. Anouilh's *Becket* (*dir.* Peter Glenville) is not intended as a factual chronicle but rather as a sort of witty historical conceit. The film follows the play closely, and Burton's characterisation goes as deep as the author permits, suggesting the change from the roistering companion of the King to the austere and flexible prelate convincingly and with moments of considerable dignity and power. Numerous sequences are visually beautiful, and for a change both sets and costumes look as if they were lived in and not hired for the period of shooting—but as a study of either history or of spiritual growth it never pretends to be other than superficial, totally ignoring such inconvenient facts of history as that of Becket being a dozen or more years older than Henry.

A Man for All Seasons is discussed in Chapter Seven, but mention may be made here of Orson Welles's mountainously impressive Wolsey and Cyril Luckham's Cranmer.

Several documentary and semi-documentary films on the lives of contemporary Popes have been issued. The earliest

Right, BECKET:
the "considerable dignity and power"
of Richard Burton in the title role

74

is probably the American Biograph's *Leo XIII in the Vatican,* made in 1900. Pathé in 1905 released a reconstruction of the death of Leo XIII and the advent of Pius X. In *The Great Catholic Festival* (1913), Pius X appeared in person. A straightforward biography of the same Pope was made in Rome in 1952, with the English actor Henry Vidon in the name part. The film takes liberty with facts in order to make points, but contains interesting details of the inner workings of the Vatican. There is an American version, very badly dubbed. *The Coronation of Pope John XXIII* (1958) is the first occasion on which the ceremony has been filmed in colour. A life of Pope John entitled *And There Came a Man* (1965, *dir.* Ermanno Olmi) uses Rod Steiger as a sort of combined stand-in and commentator. The film is an amalgam of documentary, historical collation and reconstructed event, the material being drawn from the *Giornale dell' Anima.*

4. Preachers, Evangelists, Missionaries

GEORGE LOANE TUCKER's *The Miracle Man* (1919) was supposed to have helped to break down the star system by demonstrating that films could do without names and yet make money. The system, however, made a rapid recovery. Three of the unknowns, Betty Compson, Lon Chaney and Thomas Meighan, went on to become top silent stars themselves. In fact, the player who was least heard of afterwards was the Miracle Man himself, Joseph Dowling. In the conventional eyes-uplifted-to-skies style of the period it is a convincing portrait of a faith-healer, and Dowling has a fine dignified presence. The story of petty crooks and fake cripples brought to repentance by a genuine cure is given the full emotional treatment, and the film was a great success, being considerably helped in this by the support of Christian Scientists. In one scene Thomas Meighan was required to burst into tears on being converted. He was quite unable to do so at first, but later—having started—was equally unable to stop. Loane Tucker at once turned the camera on him—and Meighan's "magnificent acting" was widely acclaimed. *The Miracle Man* was re-made in 1933 with the fine old veteran Hobart Bosworth in the title role, directed by Norman Z. McLeod.

1921 saw a curious little production entitled *The Sin Flood*, based on a forgotten stage play and inspired by the Johnstown and Dayton disasters. The story, a sort of modern Noah's Ark without animals, takes place in a saloon barred against the floodwaters owing to the premonition of a patriarchal preacher who sees the calamity as a judgment of God on the inhabitants. Closeted together in the midst of an apparently drowned world, a group of men and a girl work out their various problems, aided and scolded by the preacher until, in rising hysteria, preferring to drown quickly rather than to starve slowly, they fling open the door—revealing rain-washed but glistening pavements, and people calmly walking by. James Kirkwood is suitably gaunt and bearded as the modern Noah. Minor work though it certainly is, the final scenes leading up to the well-contrived anti-climax of the opening door, is quite memorable. It was re-made as an early talkie (*dir.* Frank Lloyd) with Robert Edeson as the preacher.

The Glorious Adventure (1922, *dir.* Stuart Blackton) was a grandiose, tedious affair, made in much publicised early colour, dealing with the plague and the fire of London and vaguely based on Harrison Ainsworth. It is worthy of mention here, however, because of the splendidly mad and prophetic figure of Solomon Eagle (Tom Haselwood) striding the streets of the capital, brazier smoking on his head, crying the Wrath to Come.

Three versions of Somerset Maugham's *Rain* have been made —the first, silent of course, in 1928. Gloria Swanson plays *Sadie Thompson* (under which title the film was released), the prostitute who has fled from San Francisco to escape arrest and now entertains the troops in the South Seas. Lionel Barrymore is the missionary who sets out to redeem her and persuade her to return to San Francisco and face her punishment. He succeeds, but in the moment of doing so gives way to his own frustrated desire, seduces her, and the following morning drowns himself. Though marred by a contrived happy ending this version, directed by Raoul Walsh, is still the best of the three, partly because of unglamorously realistic settings but chiefly because of fine performances from both stars. The second version, the only one to retain the original title of *Rain,* was made by Lewis Milestone in 1933, with Walter Huston as an impressive missionary but unable to equal Barrymore in the suggestion of the man's inner conflict. The third re-make stars Rita Hayworth and is called, perhaps significantly, *Miss Sadie Thompson* (1953, *dir.* Curtis Bernhardt). Miss Hayworth cavorts around in usual style, "sings" a song called "South Pacific Blues" and presents perhaps the least convincing convert who ever saw the Light. Faced with all this, José Ferrer looks understandably embarrassed as he fights his losing battle, and Maugham's rather obvious but bitter and quite moving monitory tale sinks without trace. According to Paul Rotha, the Will Hays office ordered the title of the 1928 version to be changed from *Rain* to *Sadie Thompson* on moral grounds. Inscrutable are the minds of moral custodians.

King Vidor's famous Negro film *Hallelujah!* appeared in 1929. It contains numerous scenes of preaching and religious ceremonies, treated without patronage or condescension. Much of the film is charming, and much exciting. In his book *A Tree is a Tree* he tells a pleasant story of how, at one moment, he had everything arranged for a river-baptism scene and was about to call "action," when he noticed a commotion by the river's edge. On inquiry, he was told that there were among the extras four ordained Baptists, who declared he was completely wrong in his staging of the ceremony. The two long lines of separated male and female candidates, which had taken a lot of expensive time to arrange, were the wrong way round—left should be right—right, left. The re-ordering took another hour of costly shooting time. Even more charming is the help he received from a local character in Tennessee named Reverend Jackson. When asked if Vidor might employ members of his congregation, Reverend Jackson said he would have to consult the Lord about that, and proceeded to do so, using his hands as the mouthpiece and receiver of a telephone. It is pleasant to record that after a long conversation the Lord was persuaded to approve, and that the same communicative method was used with equal success for the solution of other administrative problems, such as the method of payment for the congregation's services.

A film inspired by the career of the well-known woman evangelist Aimée Semple MacPherson and her Angelus Temple was directed by Frank Capra in 1931, entitled *The Miracle Woman*. It is a satirical glance at the more questionable and extravagant activities of the American religious fringe, though weakened by an unlikely reformation (through Love) at the end. Barbara Stanwyck is at her best, as the evangelist.

Also dealing with faith healing in America (in a pool in a forest this time), but without the saving graces of humour or sympathetic inquiry, *The Healer* (1935, *dir*. Reginald Barker) is just another love story with the mystical element introduced to provide an additional "angle."

A much-heralded film biography of *Brigham Young* (1940, *dir*. Henry Hathaway) disappointingly proved to be more of a conventional costume spectacle than an attempt to present the life of the great Mormon leader. Dean Jagger looks imposing and breathes fanaticism, but the film reveals little about either the man or the sect. This is a pity, because a really memorable production could surely be made of the epic journey and founding of Salt Lake City.

The film version of *Major Barbara*, Bernard Shaw's Salvation Army play on the themes of whether it is right to use the Devil's money (i.e. from armaments) in the service of God, and whether more useful work could be done outside the Army's shelter, weakens its impact by presenting the tycoon as a jolly, magnetic fellow, and by omitting much of his ruthless arguments concerning the use of new and terrible weapons on comparatively defenceless people—in this case the Chinese. On the credit side, much Shavian sermonising also disappears. The result is mildly entertaining.

A psychopathic preacher is the central character in *The Night of the Hunter* (1955), a strange and haunting film directed by Charles Laughton. The preacher tries to track down the widow of a man recently hanged for murder because he is convinced that she or her children can show him where the proceeds of her husband's robbery are concealed. God has told him to use the money for building a chapel, and to kill wicked women, if necessary, en route. He does eventually kill the widow, and later hunts the fleeing children through the moonlit countryside. They take refuge with an odd but kindly spinster (Lillian Gish), who thwarts the preacher when he arrives in pursuit. The bare bones of the story afford little idea of the beauty and terror of the film itself—the strange mixing of poetry and evil. Robert Mitchum, seemingly an odd choice, powerfully conveys the brooding fanaticism of the religious maniac.

The Inn of the Sixth Happiness (1958, *dir.* Mark Robson) purports to be the true story of Gladys Aylward, the courageous young English servant girl who became a missionary in China, the climax of the film being her hazardous and successful journey with a group of Chinese children over the Yellow River and the mountains, to safety. Unfortunately, and inevitably, a plain and inspiring tale of courage and stalwart faith has been softened and romanticised—with a love affair, a group of appealing little slant-eyed children, charmingly ragged, a big beautiful Swedish film star representing the tough little English servant, and an ending—chorus of singing child voices growing ever nearer over the hills as the procession led by Ingrid Bergman trudges towards the waiting crowds and the minister on the mission steps—all too mechanically guaranteed to bring a tear to every eye. Miss Bergman is warm, sincere and dedicated—but one knows only too well that she, of all people, cannot be allowed to fail, and the film becomes just another variant of the escape story, puffed out at times with pseudo-mystical-philosophical conversation. It dwindles in grandeur as it grows in grandiosity.

Also founded vaguely on fact, *The Saint of Devil's Island* (1960, *dir.* Douglas Cox) concerns the mission of the Salvation Army to help prisoners on Devil's Island and its part in persuading the French Government eventually to close the settlement altogether. In addition it contains a love story, a convicts' revolt, an abortive escape attempt, and Eartha Kitt.

Elmer Gantry (1960, *dir.* Richard Brooks) is a rumbustious version of Sinclair Lewis's vehement attack on commercialised, show-business revivalism. With a splendidly ranting, artificially-worked-up performance from Burt Lancaster, the film is an exciting and seemingly accurate exposure of the financial deals, the fake emotionalism, the hysterical hell-for-leather sermonising which go to make up big business evangelism. Set against Gantry's shouting and ranting is sister Sharon's quieter and more genuine group, into which he has wandered as a travelling salesman, and from which his own reputation stems. Unfortunately, however, the ending of the film seems to lose the courage of its condemnation. Sister Sharon works a "miracle," her tabernacle catches fire, she refuses to leave it, and dies. Gantry returns to the road. The entire sequence of events is suddenly arbitrary—as artificial, in fact, as the deliberately invoked religious emotion which most of the film is at pains to denounce. This is the more noticeable as it goes entirely against the character of sister Sharon which we have so far seen. Apart from this, however, the film is unfailingly interesting and often exhilarating, indulging in neither easy moral indignation nor cheap satirical sneers. In fact, it continually throws out hints that beneath all Gantry's showmanship and money-grabbing there may—perhaps—exist a genuine belief in what he preaches.

In 1965 John Ford directed *Seven Women*. It is difficult to understand the lack of interest in this haunting and beautiful film. To say that people have not wanted to go to see it is begging the question. Most of them never had the chance. The film had no major première in England, and was double-billed on release. Yet *Seven Women* is one of the very best on its subject yet made, exciting, moving, visually beautiful, amusing and inspiring, completely free from the tendentious verbosity and false sentimentality of so many pictures with a "religious" subject or background. It is superlatively acted by a distinguished cast, and shows Ford at his best. The bare story line is uncomplicated. The setting—an American mission in a lonely part of China; the year—1935; the inhabitants—a strict, lonely, embittered woman, Miss Andrews, and those working under her. These include a young girl, Emma Clark and two middle-aged women, one of whom (Florrie) is pregnant. There is also Florrie's well-meaning, weak-willed husband, Charles. Hardly an inspiring group, and the mission is already troubled by barely concealed tensions—chiefly caused by Miss Andrews in her frustration and her evident attraction towards the girl. Outside, the district is being held in terror by bandit hordes. The action throughout takes place within the walled enclosure of the little settlement, inhabited, in addition to the members, by a number of villagers and children. A doctor is awaited—impatiently by the pitiable and self-pitying Florrie. On arrival, this doctor turns out to be a young woman (superbly played by Anne Bancroft), smart, capable, cynical, worldly wise, with little time for the religious niceties and formalities of Miss Andrews's mission. In very little time the two are in conflict—not least on account of the doctor's growing friendship with Emma Clark. Internal stress is temporarily relieved by the arrival of the remnants of a British mission whose headquarters have been sacked by the marauders. They are led by Miss Binns (Flora Robson outstanding in a comparatively small role) and a Chinese woman. The entrance of the motley procession through the wide wooden gateway and across the courtyard is one of the highlights of the film. An outbreak of cholera follows. The doctor brings it under control, thus further lessening the authority of Miss Andrews, who stands around in helpless, pathetic dignity. In the face of increasing danger from the Mongols, the husband gathers together the tattered remnants of his self-respect and goes off to investigate and seek help. It is a useless and futile gesture, but the very restraint and lack of conventional coward-turned-hero sentimentality in Ford's treatment make Charles's last exit, accompanied by his wife's frenzied screams, to what we know is his death, intensely moving. The bandits trick their way into the compound by using the murdered man's car, and shut the women up in an outhouse, hoping eventually to extort ransom. Here, Florrie's labour begins, while the Mongols riot outside. From the start, the doctor stands up to them, demanding to be allowed to fetch her medical instruments—agreeing to the leader's demand that she return to him as her part of the bargain. She also obtains food for the other women. The baby is born to the accompaniment of curses from the almost insane Miss Andrews. The fact that such potentially melodramatic and embarrassing scenes remain true and convincing is largely due to Margaret Leighton's hypnotic performance. In the end, the doctor even manages to arrange for the others to leave the mission safely, and they trundle away, a pathetic band, over the bumpy road. The doctor dresses in Chinese clothes, goes to the bandit leader's room, and manages to poison both their glasses of wine from her store of medicines. They drink to each other and, with a friendly smile, she tells the uncomprehending Mongol succinctly what she thinks of him. "You bastard!" she says, and, as he slumps on the floor, she drains her own glass. Ford's attitude to the missionaries, and to the God they not very efficiently represent, is ambiguous. Certainly they seem to have done little enough "good" by their efforts, even taking the word at their own evaluation. The only character who achieves anything very positive is the drinking, smoking (before grace), blaspheming doctor. But Ford's deeply imaginative treatment, the cool compassion which envelops the whole film, make the question of their usefulness, their "worth" somehow immaterial. They are *people*—who went or drifted into this strange lonely corner of a missionary's work, and there lived their lives. That may be little enough, but we feel as the film draws to an end that it is all that needs to be said. It is a favourite of Ford's among his own films.

As a fictional account of early missionaries in Polynesia, *Hawaii* (1966, *dir.* George Roy Hill) suffers from its proportions—a huge spectacular, with outsize screen and "cast of thousands." Inevitably much time is taken up with large set pieces—in particular a well-staged but interminable storm on the journey from New England. However, when these are allowed for, much of interest remains, and one set piece at any rate, the tremendous hurricane which sweeps the island, wrecking the new church and reducing the proud preacher to a cowering, dust-covered heap, has both a symbolic and a dramatic part in the action of the story. This depicts the slow, painful change in the character of Abner Hale, from a callow, arrogant and self-opinionated young man to a worn, lonely figure who at the very last is beginning to learn something of humility and compassion. This is no easy spiritual growth. Abner's struggle, against the islanders and even more against himself, is tough and bitter, as he rewards their early welcome by attempting to force them into the straitjacket of his own narrow beliefs. Max von Sydow manages to make Abner un-

This page and right, HAWAII:
Max von Sydow as
the proud preacher, Abner Hale

derstandable, almost likeable, even at his most stiff-necked and arrogant, and commands sympathy at the end without resorting to any Dickensian "crusty-lovable-old-codger" tricks. He communicates throughout his sense of "mission," and his lean, lanky, stove-pipe hatted figure survives in the memory long after the wide-screen storms and milling extras have become indistinguishable among those of a score of similar spectacles.

In 1968 the pop singer Cliff Richard appeared in *Two a*

HAWAII:
Max von Sydow

Penny (*dir.* James F. Collier), a well-meaning but ingenuous story of religious conversion through the evangelism of Billy Graham—who is shown in action at one of his mammoth meetings. Ann Holloway portrays a young girl's conversion convincingly, and sincerity shines from every frame, but scenes such as the religious discussions between parson and "young people" are facile and without bite, and the film contains several moments of really notable mawkishness.

88

5. Monks and Nuns

A LTHOUGH PORTRAYALS OF MONKS and the monastic life are much less frequent than those of the priesthood, several actresses have had an irresistible urge to don the nun's robes and veil, even if in the majority of cases the stories have been only superficially concerned with the religious aspect. Generally they make use of the retreat to solve a triangular problem, or afford a Grand Renunciation scene. An early example is *The White Sister*, first filmed in 1915 by Essanay, with Viola Allen. The great silent star Francis X. Bushman (*Ben Hur*'s Messala) reputedly walked out of the studio when asked to play opposite her in support, and Richard Travers took his place. The most famous version was that made by Inspiration in 1924, starring Lillian Gish and most sensitively directed by Henry King. Miss Gish gives one of her best performances as the young girl torn between her call to a life of religious dedication and her love for a young French officer—Ronald Colman is his first American role. It all appears very simple and naïve now, but the contrast between Lillian Gish's fragile beauty and her iron determination to follow her conscience made it the tear-jerker of its day. It was re-made with sound in 1933 but, despite a touching and sincere performance from Helen Hayes, the time and the spirit had passed. A Mexican version, *La Hermana Blanca*, was produced in 1960, directed by Tito Davison.

As Colin Wilson remarks in his book *Rasputin and the Fall of the Romanovs*, Grigory Rasputin was "a man who was obsessed by religion—a Messianic self-belief was his mainspring, not sexual voracity or a will to political power." Not unexpectedly, the various film versions of his life have dwelt mainly on the last two—and particularly the former. He made what seems to be his first cinematic appearance in 1917, in

a World production entitled *Rasputin, the Black Monk* (most of the films concerned find a sensational subtitle irresistible). Montagu Love played the name part, and stills show a make-up very much modified from the well-known photographs—the hair neatly bobbed and the tangled yards of whiskers trimmed to a neat moustache and imperial—a gentleman's monk, in fact. A silent Russian *Rasputin* came out in 1929 (*dir.* Nikolai Larin) with Gregor Chmara; a German one in 1930 (*dir.* Adolf Trotz) with Conrad Veidt; and yet another in the same year with Martin Berger as director and Nikolai Malikoff starring. Of this group, Veidt's appears to have been the most significant, compelling considerable sympathy for the character. Only two years later the appearance of all three Barrymores at once in M-G-M's *Rasputin and the Empress* (*dir.* Richard Boleslavski, alternative title *Rasputin—the Mad Monk*) exhausted this particular market for six years, until, in 1938, Harry Bauer appeared in a French version called, modestly, *Rasputin.* The famous Metro picture (Lionel Barrymore as Rasputin, John as a pseudonymous Prince Yousupoff, Ethel as the Empress—and Ralph Morgan, in far the best likeness, as the Czar) came out in a furore of publicity; and its alleged distortions of fact, in which it is certainly not alone, led to the further excitements of subsequent lawsuits. Lionel Barrymore's performance is powerful and theatrical—his agonising, long-drawn death scene is a *tour-de-force*. Ethel Barrymore's comment to a friend years later, after watching the film on television, was: "I thought I was pretty good, but what those two boys were up to I'll never know." Bauer is reportedly excellent in the less embellished French film. Another came from France in 1954, directed by Georges Combret and featuring Pierre Brasseur and Isa Miranda, and one of the de-

Left, Lillian Gish in THE WHITE SISTER

plorably dubbed Italian sub-spectacles turned up (and was generally turned down) in 1960, with Edmund Purdom. This was called *Nights of Rasputin* and directed by Pierre Chenal. Surprisingly, it follows historical events (at least those it chooses to select, which are foreseeable) with reasonable accuracy, but it is a flat and aimless affair and Purdom's monk would never have reached either the heights or the depths attained by the man he portrays. The same cannot be held against Christopher Lee in Hammer's 1965 version, *Rasputin— The Mad Monk* (once more), which is directed by Don Sharp. Although the atmosphere and conditions of pre-Revolutionary Russia are conspicuous by their absence, the facts of history manipulated to serve the ends of a piece of fiction, and a few typical Hammer horrors determinedly dragged in, the film is well worth seeing for Lee's performance alone. Both in appearance and action it is a powerful one. The Czar, incredibly, never appears at all.

The most recent candidate in the Rasputin stakes is Gert Frobe in *J'ai tué Rasputin* (*dir.* Robert Hossein). Perhaps one day a film will explore the religious, political and superstitious obsessions of those all-important Russian years which helped to bring about Rasputin's astounding career—in addition to the scandals, orgies and corruption which culminated in the melodramatics of his appalling death.

Another famous love-versus-cloister story is *The Garden of Allah*, Robert Hichens's novel about a renegade Trappist monk in North Africa who is persuaded to return (and Renounce) by the woman he has met and grown to love. It was first filmed in 1917 with Thomas Santschi and Helen Ware, and again in 1928 with Ivan Petrovich and Alice Terry, the latter giving a beautiful, if rather cold performance under the direction of her husband Rex Ingram, not to be confused with De Lawd in *The Green Pastures*. In the 1936 edition (*dir.* Richard

Boleslavski) Charles Boyer plays the monk with notable sincerity. The film contains absurdities and dramatic *clichés*: Aubrey Smith as a Catholic priest suggesting inevitably the Captain of the English eleven, Marlene Dietrich's gloved hand waving the monk farewell from a carriage window as from a coronation coach, the monastery wine of which the monk alone knows the secret—thus making his return advantageous on material as well as spiritual grounds. Despite all this, something of a man's agonised confrontation with his destiny comes across in Boyer's performance.

Martinez Sierra's gentle comedy, *The Cradle Song*, has been accused of presenting a sentimental view of convent life. The story is simple in the extreme. An abandoned baby girl is found in a basket outside the gate, taken in and cared for. Eighteen years later, she leaves to marry the man she loves. The novice who found and nursed her throughout is the person chiefly affected, but the impact on all the sisters is sketched in. Admittedly all the stereotypes are there: the sharp-tongued nun, the apparently harsh but really soft-hearted nun, the calm, withdrawn nun, the placid, sweet nun, the young nun with unfulfilled maternal instincts, the middle-aged nun with unfulfilled maternal instincts, the crusty old nun, the school-girlish young nun. Admittedly, too, the less picturesque psychological stresses of conventual life are barely touched upon. In addition the original play, with its sharp division into two acts—the interval moving the action on eighteen years—is dramatically more satisfactory than the continuously flowing film. Nevertheless the latter has enormous charm, sentiment without sentimentality, and, aided by a fine cast led by Dorothea Wieck, presents a compelling picture of the quiet calm of the withdrawn life.

To appreciate the dignity and integrity of a film such as *The Cradle Song*, despite its soft centre, one has only to consider what has been perpetrated in other pictures of nuns and nunneries. *The Angelus* (1937, *dir.* Thomas Bentley) tells of a nun who leaves her convent to aid the marriage of a man who is in love with her niece. *Bonaventure* (titled in the United States *Thunder on the Hill*)—even less probable—concerns the activities of a nun-detective who saves a girl from a miscarriage of justice when floods interrupt her journey to prison and cause her to seek refuge in an East Anglian convent. After such unusual events as the attempted murder of the sister by the real murderer for whom the fleeing girl is taking the rap, she (the sister) returns to her devotions fortified by the knowledge that she has fulfilled a large part of her purpose, as designed by God, on earth. This effort was directed by Douglas Sirk and released in 1951. 1957 must shoulder the responsibility for *Heaven Knows, Mr. Allison* (*dir.* John Huston) and *The Miracle* (*dir.* Irving Rapper). The former, telling the tale of a young nun and a tough American marine corporal forced to live together—in the nicest possible sense—on a Pacific island when it is occupied by the Japanese during the Second World War, at least has the advantage of some sharp Huston direction, a certain unsubtle but ironic humour, and good acting from Deborah Kerr and Robert Mitchum. *The Miracle* presents Carroll Baker as a Spanish sister during the Peninsular Wars and concerns a statue of the Virgin Mary which jumps off its pedestal, dresses up in Miss Baker's habit while the latter is running after an English officer she has fallen for, and helps to keep matters going on her (Miss Baker's) behalf. After numerous peculiar proceedings, the nun returns to her convent, the Virgin Mary to her pedestal, and presumably all, except perhaps the officer, live happily ever afterwards.

After this it is a relief to turn back to 1940 and Edward G. Robinson in *Brother Orchid* (*dir.* Lloyd Bacon). He appears as a hunted gangster who is taken into a monastery in a collapsed condition and there resuscitated. He thereupon stays on as a novice, taking the name of the film's title. It is an odd, quirky, tough little picture—undoubtedly not to be relied on as a picture of monastic life—but providing Robinson with a tartly comic characterisation.

Les Anges du Péché (1943) is Robert Bresson's first full-length film (his original title for it had been *Béthanie,* but the producers knew better). The story was suggested to him by a Dominican Brother, Father R. P. Bruckberger, and the setting is a convent of the Dominican Order, the Sisters of Bethany, to which are admitted both young girls straight from their families, and ex-convicts on their release from prison. Soon, it was said, there would be no apparent difference between the two categories. The film deals with the relationship between a girl from each of them. The former, Anne-Marie, comes from a secure, comfortable home, knowing little of the world outside. The latter, Thérèse, released from prison after serving an unjust sentence, shoots the man responsible and then enters the convent for refuge. Both become novices. Anne-Marie feels a slightly unnatural and desperate necessity to befriend Thérèse and help her to accept the disciplines of the religious life. Thérèse resists both Anne-Marie's friendship and her reformative efforts. Anne-Marie's actions now appear not so simple as at first sight. She seems as much drawn by fascination as determined to destroy the wickedness of life as she sees it in Thérèse. Eventually the latter's continual rejections provoke a nervous crisis in Anne-Marie. She has outbursts of anger and defiance. She becomes arrogant. Brought under discipline, she refuses to perform a penance, and is dismissed from the convent. She haunts the buildings, is found in the grounds one night, utterly exhausted, and is readmitted. She is now too weak to read her vows,

95

however, and Thérèse performs this service for her, afterwards giving herself up to the police. Bresson treats this potentially lurid story with absolute sobriety and rigorous control —convincingly suggesting the claustrophobic life, actual and metaphorical, of the convent; the tensions, collective and individual, to which the inhabitants may be subject; and, over all, the austere, cool, enveloping permanence of the Order. In the end the two girls have, as suggested, almost changed places. Bresson had considerable difficulty in arousing interest in the production of his film, but in the end was fortunate enough to be given a relatively free hand. The result is a re-

Anglo-Catholic nuns in the Himalayas:
a beautifully composed still from BLACK NARCISSUS

ligious film of a grave, ascetic beauty, with wonderful black-and-white photography and a number of performances of great subtlety and understanding.

To 1947 belongs Michael Powell's and Emeric Pressburger's *Black Narcissus*. As usual, Powell and Pressburger incurred certain critical censure on the grounds of vulgarity and sensationalism, but in fact this is a ravishingly beautiful film, and as sincere in feeling as many higher-claiming religious epics, even if some of the situations (e.g. "frustrated" sister going off her head) are becoming familiar. The story deals with the trials and tribulations of a small group of Anglo-Catholic nuns who open a hospital-cum-school in the Himalayas. More emphasis is laid on personal problems than on the larger religious issues, and there is a certain artificiality of atmosphere—but a genuine sense of poetry illuminates the whole film, which is continuously interesting and original. Many individual shots, such as the start of the rains, with great drops splashing on the enormous green leaves, are visually unforgettable. There are also some memorable performances from Deborah Kerr, Flora Robson, Jean Simmons and, as the tormented woman, Kathleen Byron.

In *Come to the Stable* (1949, *dir.* Henry Koster), two nuns arrive in New England from France in order to fulfil a vow made during the war that they would build a sanitorium for children. They turn up at a village named Bethlehem and find—the Holy Family sitting round a manger. Understandably puzzled by this fortunate collection of omens, they elicit the more prosaic truth that the group is posing for Elsa Lanchester to paint a picture, and is composed of very earthly villagers. The task of the nuns would appear to be fraught with difficulties, but confronted by the pretty faces and indestructible self-satisfaction of Loretta Young and Celeste Holm all problems melt shamefacedly away, and everything becomes saccharine and light. The most caustic criticism probably does less harm to the object of its attack than this sort of pink lampshade cosiness.

A silent film on *Luther* was made in Germany by Hans Kyser in 1928, with Eugene Klöpfer playing the title role, but the most ambitious attempt was the Louis de Rochemont production in 1953, directed by Irving Pichel. It was made with the co-operation of the Lutheran Church Productions, Inc., and filmed on locations in Western Germany. It was banned in Quebec, and found unacceptable by the American National League of Decency! The story follows Luther from the moment when he announces his decision to leave his law studies at Erfurt University and seek peace of mind and soul in a monastery. Haunted by a sense of guilt and sin, he is unable to settle, and is eventually sent back to the University by the Vicar, von Staupitz, and later despatched on a pilgrimage to Rome. After running into trouble over his suggestion that the Bible should be translated into the vernacular, he becomes a doctor of theology at Wittenberg. From there the film follows his life and work until the publication of the Augsburg Confession, and ends with Luther giving thanks in Church and with the congregation singing the wonderful Reformation Anthem, "Ein' feste Burg ist unser Gott." Avoiding melodramatics to the point of occasional flatness, the film at other points touches greatness—notably in the tremendous portrayal by Niall MacGinnis, whose great climaxes, such as the heroic refusal to recant, are overwhelming in their power and attack. Indeed, the entire film has a truth and nobility which more than compensate for any lack of superficial excitements.

The Burmese Harp (*Biruma No Tategoto*, directed by Kon Ichikawa) tells the story of a young Japanese private in Burma who is nursed back from near-death by a Buddhist monk, returns wearing one. of the monk's robes, and, on seeing a

Nuns under discipline: Audrey Hepburn in THE NUN'S STORY

memorial service to the Unknown Japanese Warrior held by some English soldiers and nurses, is overcome by a sense of vocation to honour the unknown dead by burying them. Presented in an epic, stylised manner rather than naturalistically, as an illustration of the strength of vocation in a world of weakness and despair, the film is universal in its religious significance.

The Nun's Story (1958, *dir.* Fred Zinnemann) is a serious and fairly uncompromising study of a young Belgian nursing sister's attempt to come to terms with the rules of the convent

99

she has entered. After encountering many problems and set-backs, she is sent out to Africa, has to resist her love for the doctor under whom she works, returns to the convent and finally, unable to submit to the mental and physical discipline required, returns to the outside world. The story is a true one: the issues are not shirked, and the fact that the problems are worked out intellectually rather than dramatically (though there are several scenes of quite violent action), adds to the unusual quality of an always interesting, if not wholly successful, film. The need for courage and sacrifice in some aspects of a nursing sister's work—among lepers, among the insane—is brought out with horrifying realism. Almost as difficult for a young girl to suffer, the seeming pettiness and high-school restrictions of much convent life are equally frankly presented. The film is well served by its cast—notably Audrey Hepburn, Edith Evans and Peter Finch.

The Carmelites (1959, *dir.* R. L. Bruckberger, Philippe Agostini) is set in the period of the French Revolution and purports to be an accurate picture of convent life during those tumultuous years. Jeanne Moreau's performance as one of the nuns, has been commended.

In 1960 Alberto Lattuada directed *The Novice* (*La Novizia*), a highly sensational story of a girl who becomes infatuated with her mother's lover and wants to marry him. When he returns to her mother, the girl kills him and hopes to find sanctuary under the veil. The story comes out when, as she is about to take her vows, she faints after hearing a sermon preached by her confessor. I can find no trace of the film's release in England, but a French critic describes Pascale Petit (the novice) as exquisite and diabolical, and the story as the

Right, nuns possessed:
MOTHER JOAN OF THE ANGELS

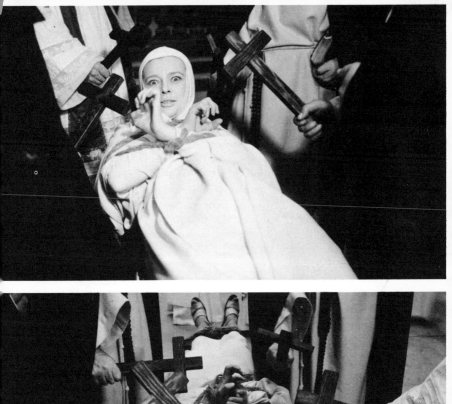

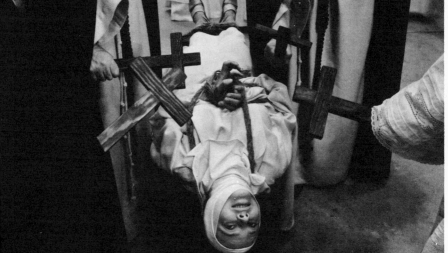

exact equivalent of the "pseudo-moral libidinous romances read by the eighteenth-century aristocracy."

A Polish film of major interest, also appearing in 1960, is *Mother Joan of the Angels*—alternatively, since sensationalism must be shoved into a title by hook or by crook, *The Devil and the Nun*—directed by Jerzy Kawalerowicz. It won the Special Jury prize at the 1961 Cannes Festival, and is based on the demoniac possession of the nuns of Loudun in Seventeenth century France—though the actual story is set in Poland and derived from a Polish novel. Mother Joan, together with all the sisters under her save one, are rumoured to have become possessed by devils. The parish priest has been burnt at the stake for having set the devils free, and all attempts to exorcise them by solemn public ceremonies appear to have failed. The bishop then sends an ascetic Abbé, Father Joseph Suryn, who decides to try other methods, relying on the power of secluded prayer. Instead of the raving maniac he has been led to expect, he discovers in Mother Joan a calm and handsome woman, but one ruled by spiritual arrogance, which he considers it is his duty to subdue. These approaches also fail to exorcise the evil, and in time Father Suryn finds himself drawn to Mother Joan by more earthly sentiments. A rabbi to whom he goes for advice proves little help—suggesting the trouble might be not so much the presence of demons as the absence of angels. "The angel has left Mother Joan and she remains alone—free to be herself. It is, perhaps, the more natural state?" Despairingly, Father Joseph puts up a trellis in the upper room to separate himself from Mother Joan, but this only increases the tension between them. He concludes that the devils have entered into himself also. Meanwhile the unaffected nun has fled from the convent with

Right: MOTHER JOAN OF THE ANGELS

a supposed nobleman. He, after promising to take her away and care for her, leaves her abandoned. Father Joseph, tormented beyond endurance, decides to take to himself all the sins and devils rampant in the convent, and deliberately kills two innocent people in a nearby tavern. There he meets the deserted sister and sends her back to inform Mother Joan of the crime he has committed for love of her, and because of his desire to save her and the others. Kawalerowicz has said, "My film is a protestation against the fetters imposed on man from outside, whether Catholic or not." Though undoubtedly condemnatory of certain aspects of the enclosed religious life, it might well be regarded as having equal political significance. The director, however, has also stated, "I am an atheist, but I have not intended to make a film of religious propaganda —nor, in fact, of propaganda of any kind." The production is distinguished by the austere beauty of its compositions, its magnificent photography (in few films can one so nearly *feel* the textures of wood and stone), and the inspired playing of its cast.

Bruno Paolinelli's *The Novice* (*La Suora Giovane*, 1964), tells the story of love between a forty-year-old man and a young nun. The film treats the delicate situation with compassion but without sentimentality, and the result is both credible and touching.

There are no torments in *The Lilies of the Field* (1963, *dir.* Ralph Nelson). In the United States South a coloured man helps a party of East European refugee nuns to build a chapel —teaching them English at the same time—then passes on. The over-simplifications are obvious. Every world problem touched on (and most of them are) may be solved by simple faith. The film, however, has a pleasant lack of pretension, and the rather obvious "charm" is saved from cloying by a certain tartness of approach.

104

No tartness at all sharpens the sweetness of the vocalising sisters of *The Sound of Music* (1965, *dir.* Robert Wise); and the saga of the singing nuns reaches its apogee in—simply— *The Singing Nun* (1965, *dir.* Henry Koster), in which Sister Ann (Debbie Reynolds) not only sings, but plays the guitar and rides on a scooter—not, regrettably, all at the same time.

The Trouble with Angels (1966, *dir.* Ida Lupino) is a Convent School Story, with Hayley Mills, having distinguished herself as the "Worst Girl in the Form," deciding to take the veil at the end of her last term. The death of one of the sisters is ruthlessly engineered to bring about this desirable change, after more than one hundred minutes of schoolgirl high jinks and distracted teaching nuns. A possible alternative title might be "Do not send your daughter to a Convent, Mrs. Worthington"—even one which has Gypsy Rose Lee as a dancing mistress. A sequel in the same vein is promised, following its success: *Where Angels Go—Trouble Follows.*

Though in general we are not concerned with short films— and the nun in question is not even a genuine one—mention must be made of the charming and original *Scene Nun—Take One,* written, directed and produced by Maurice Hatton. The string of episodes, too slight to be called a story, concerns the adventures of a young actress playing a nun in a film who has a tiff with her director, goes off in a rage, and is taken by the public she encounters for the genuine article. Shot on location, often with a hidden camera, in pubs, a department store, a children's playground, at a fashion-photography session, a cinema queue (where she joins in an Oriental dance with three buskers), and numerous other places, the film has a gaiety and warmth which, together with Susannah York's enchanting performance, are irresistible. Unlike some shorts which one encounters time and again in supporting programmes, *Scene Nun—Take One* is always welcome, if only

Enchanting pseudo-nun . . . .

for the pleasure of again seeing Miss York, in a high-angle shot, leading a procession of dancing school children to the music of the "Messiah"; perching on top of a fireman's ladder holding out her crucifix in an attempt to dissuade a man from jumping off a roof; running riot in a West End store, trying on a variety of hats over her veil, to the astonishment of the shoppers; joining with the models in their fashion posing; careering around in a two-seater with an unsuccessful crook; doing her best to cope with a weeping Italian child, gravely and compassionately, then finishing up by losing her temper and shouting at her. . . . A moral is offered at the end: "When you're pretending to be something you're not, make sure the others are pretending too"—but in truth this exhilarating little film needs no further justification than its own tonic qualities.

1967 saw the first showing in England of Jacques Rivette's

. . . . *Susannah York in* SCENE NUN—TAKE ONE

much banned film of Diderot's classic *Suzanne Simonin, La Religieuse de Diderot* (*La Religieuse*). The novel was written in the first person as a series of letters. Rivette adopts a less subjective approach, but otherwise follows the story, or rather, series of episodes, fairly closely. The young girl, Suzanna, is forced into a convent because there is not enough money left in the family to provide her with the dowry necessary to get her married off. She refuses to take her vows, is sent home in disgrace and browbeaten until she submits. At Longchamp Convent she is at first treated with sympathy despite her lack of any sense of vocation—but after the Mother Superior's death and replacement by a harsh and rigid disciplinarian, she is hounded and degraded. After suffering humiliation and actual physical cruelty she appeals through a lawyer for release. This is refused, but she is transferred to

107

another convent. This proves to be a complete contrast—altogether of this world. Fun and games, literally, abound. The Mother Superior, based by Diderot on a real person, is a Lesbian, and falls in love with Suzanne. Eventually, with

Nun under discipline: Anna Karina in LA RELIGIEUSE

the aid of a priest who was himself forced into the religious life, she escapes into the outside world. At once he assaults her, and she runs away—finding work as a laundry girl. Eventually she is lured into a brothel and, rather than submit to the advances of the visitors, kills herself by leaping from a window. Cases of this sort were not uncommon in the period Diderot describes, and one may presume that his accounts of convent life at the time are reasonably accurate. The first part of the film is shot in cool, austere colour—the chipped stone walls and tiled floors of the building forming harshly symbolic contrasts to the vulnerable human flesh inhabiting it. The difference between this setting and the lush decadence of the second half is accentuated with startling effectiveness. If the latter seems less convincing it is partly due to the difficulty of believing that such places existed. The film has been adversely criticised in some quarters for "holding nothing for the present world," as if the value of any adaptation of a work of earlier years must be judged by how effectively it has been distorted to throw light on contemporary problems. Such criticism is not only unsound in general (re-creation is as valid as re-interpretation), but in this particular instance misguided also. *La Religieuse* is not only a protest against moral and physical oppression as a whole and at any time, but also an illustration of the fact that—as Elliott Stein neatly puts it in his full account of the film's adventures (*Sight and Sound,* Summer 1966)—"when religious life is not the result of spontaneous engagement it can lead to depravity." It has been held also against Anna Karina that she is not the Anna Karina of Jean-Luc Godard. Granted—but her blank, withdrawn passivity is precisely what one might expect from a girl who from the age of sixteen has been treated with appalling inhumanity.

6. Churches

As Leslie Halliwell points out in *The Filmgoer's Companion*, churches have "provided a setting for many pretty secular-minded films." A number, however, are worth a mention in this book, either intrinsically as settings, or as providing a symbolic commentary on the action. One of the largest and most famous sets of all was the reproduction of the Cathedral *façade* for the 1924 version of *The Hunchback of Notre Dame*. It remained a landmark of the Universal lot for months after the film was completed, and was used by Lon Chaney again in *The Phantom of the Opera* as he raced from the Opera House to the Seine in his final flight.

A documentary on this Cathedral, *Notre Dame de Paris* was made as early as 1911 (*dir*. Capellani), and another by Georges Franju in 1956. Franju's short film (*Notre Dame, Cathédrale de Paris*) is a classic example of ambiguity, and of the subjectivity of criticism. The approach, as commissioned by the producers, is outwardly factual, representing the edifice as seen in winter, summer and autumn. According to the belief behind the eye of the beholder it can be seen either as a "study of the architecture [blended] with a mood of religious . . . mysticism, the contrast of changing seasons and motionless stones and statues [suggesting] a feeling of eternity," or as "sad, dead spaces" under which "the tracking camera reveals ranks and files of empty chairs, like the skeletal backbone of a prehistoric monster." The latter is from Raymond Durgnat's detailed study of the director (*Franju*, Studio Vista, 1968) in which he also quotes a "pious spectator" who remarked to Franju's wife that "one can sense Franju is a devout Catholic, one understands that he is saying 'Look at those seats, where thousands of believers will come to pray.'"

Notably impressive are von Stroheim's churches particularly

110

in *The Wedding March* (1927), where the baroque imagery and decoration of the huge building lour over the small plain figure of the violinist's daughter; von Sternberg's in *The Scarlet Empress* (1934); and the great Russian edifices in Eisenstein's *Ivan the Terrible* (1942–6). The Cathedral setting of Becket's murder is used with great effect by Peter Glenville in *Becket,* while the 1951 version of Eliot's play on the Archbishop was filmed entirely in St. John's Church, St. John's Wood.

A church setting was used ironically by Ernst Lubitsch to point the theme of his anti-war film *The Man I Killed* (1932). As priest and congregation offer thanksgiving for peace the camera slowly descends from a high-angle shot until it comes to rest in a huge close-up of the gleaming sword scabbards of the rows of kneeling brass-hats in the pews. (Later in the same film a victory parade is filmed through the open space left by the amputated leg of a wounded private standing with his crutches by the roadside.)

Churches as symbols are frequently used: in the 1923 *Ten Commandments* the collapse of the Cathedral brings retribution for the sin of greed and theft; in *Hawaii* the destruction of his new building humbles and rebukes the arrogant missionary; in John Ford's *The Hurricane,* the tiny church is the last building to collapse in the teeth of the storm; in *The Given Word* (1962, *dir.* Anselmo Duarte) the massive edifice on its towering steps symbolises the unyielding obduracy sometimes displayed by the Church itself. In the tender, beautiful and underrated *Sundays and Cybele* 1962, (*dir.* Serge Bourguignon), Pierre, having conquered his vertigo, climbs the church steeple to collect the weather-vane for the little girl in exchange for her name—and brings tragedy to them both. In *Far from the Madding Crowd* (1967, *dir.* John Schlesinger), though the church as a focal point of Nineteenth century village life is insufficiently emphasised, the grotesque black outlines of the hovering rain-spouts provide one of the few moments in the film where the sense of a watching Destiny—Hardy's President of the Immortals at his sport—is felt.

The church as refuge is found in films as far apart as John Ford's *The Informer* (1935), with Gypo seeking sanctuary wherein to die, and the science-fiction *War of the Worlds* (1953, *dir*. Byron Haskin), with its panic-stricken crowds filling the building to hide from the invading Martians. In *No Down Payment* (1957, *dir*. Martin Ritt) it is used, perhaps ironically, as an all too facile means of solving marital and material problems.

It has also harboured evil—sensationally in *The Quatermass Experiment* (1955, *dir*. Val Guest) with a Monster in the roof of Westminster Abbey—more subtly and fearfully in *Le Corbeau* (1943, *dir*. Henri-Georges Clouzot) as the anonymous letter which is to restart the train of terror and destruction flutters slowly from the rafters over the heads of the doomed congregation. Hitchcock has long made use of the extra dimension added to fear and suspense in a consecrated setting: the Westminster Cathedral tower in *Foreign Correspondent* (1940), the seedy little East London chapel in *The Man Who Knew Too Much* (1934), the old Californian Mission in *Vertigo* (1958), the Swiss church in *The Secret Agent* (1936) with the dead man's body depressing an organ note which echoes unceasingly and unnervingly through the building.

Among other memorable settings in films not primarily concerned with religious matters may be noted the underground chapel in *Metropolis* (1926, *dir*. Fritz Lang) where the worshippers gather in secret and the robot girl takes on the likeness of the saintly Maria and incites them to revolt and destroy; the Western chapel in *High Noon* (1952, *dir*.

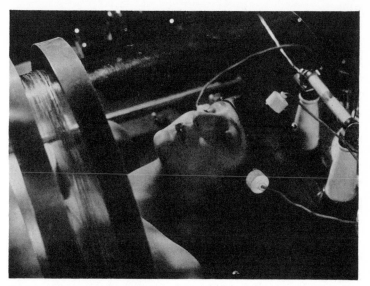

Robot girl—METROPOLIS

Fred Zinnemann) in which the practical problems of how to combat the expected villains break rudely in on the theoretical preaching of religion, with uncomfortably revealing results; the beautiful little Alpine church in the opening sequence of a fairly routine thriller *The Double Man* (1967, *dir.* Franklin J. Schaffner); the oddly impressive little tent housing the gathering of the "fringe" sect at the end of Roger Corman's macabre *Man with the X-Ray Eyes* (1963)—to mention but a few.

7. Saints, Visionaries, Legends and Miracles

OTHER THAN CHRIST HIMSELF, St. Joan of Arc has probably figured in more films than any other historical figure—with Rasputin and Napoleon as possible runners-up! It seems likely that the earliest was Pathé's *Joan of Arc* (1898, *dir.* Georges Hatot), and Méliès followed in 1900 with "a grand spectacle in twelve tableaux, and about five-hundred characters in superb costumes." Louise d'Alcy appeared as Joan in the latter version. Both Pathé and the Italian Cines company brought out films in 1908, and Italy repeated the experiment in 1913 with Maria Jacobini, directed by Nino Oxilia. As might be expected, Cecil B. DeMille was fairly early on the scene with *Joan the Woman* (1917) with the Opera singer Geraldine Farrar. Though he had made over twenty films already, this might be regarded as the first of his big "historical" spectacles. It received considerable praise, arousing favourable comment from such people as Louis Delluc, who admired in particular the processional entry into Rheims, and even resulted in the director being hailed as "the Michelangelo of the screen." DeMille's stated intention was to "emphasise the humanity of Joan of Arc rather than project the conventional image of a saint." A special suit of silver armour was constructed for Miss Farrar, because it was lighter than any other metal, and, as DeMille proudly states, "*real* fire and a *real* stake were used." The film's appearance shortly preceded America's entry into the First World War and was regarded as pro-French propaganda. Presumably to increase this effect, DeMille tacked on an unfortunate prologue and epilogue of contemporary trench warfare—but realised later that this was a dramatic error. He also incurred hostile criticism in some ecclesiastical quarters for the allegedly unflattering portrayal of certain church dignitaries, and a silly suggestion from Alexander Woollcott that Mae Marsh would have been a better choice than Geraldine Farrar because she was "more ethereal."

Eleven years later came the most famous of all the Joan films—indeed one of the most famous films of any kind—Carl Dreyer's *The Passion of Joan of Arc*. It originated in an offer from the Société Générale de Films to Dreyer, that he should choose one of three great women on which to make a great film—Catherine de Medici, Marie Antoinette, Joan of Arc. The production cost about £50,000 and opened in Copenhagen on April 21, 1928. In a full account of the making of the picture, Ebbe Neergaard points out some interesting comparisons. The film, from start of script to final completion, took one and a half years. Joan's trial also took one and a half years. In the film this is condensed to two hours, approximately the running time of the film. The action takes place within the precincts of the castle at Rouen. The classic unities are thus preserved. The whole set is built as one large unit, and painted pink to give it a grey effect against the sky.

As is well-known, the great proportion of the film is shot in close-ups, often huge, and none of the participants wear make-up. It is probable that never before, and seldom since, has the human face, in all its revealing and concealing mobility, been studied so relentlessly. For minute after minute we are shown the tragedy, pity, suffering, compassion, corruption, nobility, understanding and stupidity of those two hours through the expressions of the protagonists. Particularly unforgettable is the beautiful, ascetic face of the young monk (Antonin Artaud, referred to on p. 57), which seems to embody in itself all the paradoxical comfort, terror, pride and humility of the mediaeval church. In highly effective contrast —not always so fully appreciated—are those occasions when

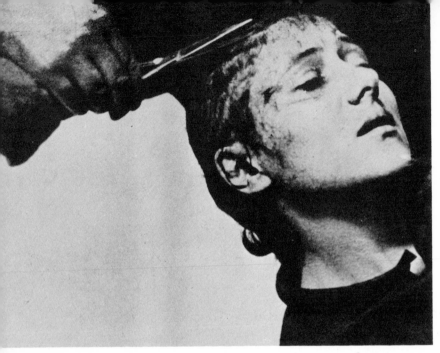

One of the great performances of screen history . . . .

Dreyer draws back from his close-ups, such as Joan's slow, heavy retirement from her preliminary examination.

The costumes are cunningly contrived to look correct without dropping an alienating veil of "mediaevalism" between the events depicted and our involvement in them. The Earl of Warwick, for instance, does not look unlike a member of the N.F.S. in the last war, and yet also remains entirely in period.

Falconetti's Joan is one of the great performances of screen history, "inspired" in the true sense of that much-abused word. Both the human weakness and the spiritual strength of the

116

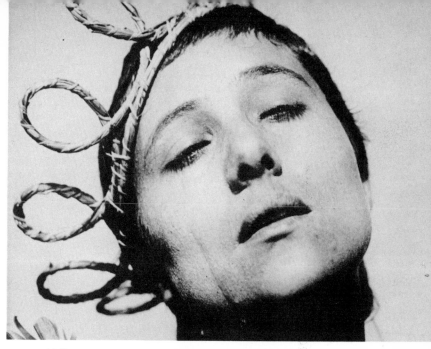

. . . . Falconetti in THE PASSION OF JOAN OF ARC

girl receive their full emphasis—neither is underlined to the detriment of the other, as often happens. Consequently her two main crises—her confession of heresy, and her recantation when, crouching alone in her cell, she sees a guard sweeping up the crown of reeds which is the symbol of her Passion —both these become wholly convincing. A disservice has been done to Falconetti in the suggestion that she is a sort of Trilby to Dreyer's Svengali, a receptive but empty vessel into which he poured his own conceptions. In fact, it is a collaboration and a partnership of the most productive kind.

117

The film is roughly divided into three parts—the installation of the tribunal; the trial; the recantation and execution. Throughout it induces, even today seen in prints inevitably scratched and imperfect, the strongest sense of involvement—of undergoing rather than watching a spiritual experience. On the last occasion I saw the film, the pianist stopped playing altogether at the moment when Joan is receiving her final communion. For several minutes there was complete silence—a silence much deeper than that of a noiseless sequence in a sound film, a silence absolutely unbroken by anyone present. The whole modern world of scientific expertise and cynicism

THE PASSION OF JOAN OF ARC:
Antonin Artaud as the young monk

receded before this forty-year-old cinematic representation of an ancient Mystery. The closing sequence of Joan's death, with its bustle, its clattering preparations as the soldiers prepare to meet trouble, its billowing smoke and grotesque weeping crowds, its sense of business-like, solemn urgency, its long agony and final catastrophe—induce in the viewer an ultimate emptiness, a draining of the emotions such as may be experienced at the close of a fine production of Shakespearian or Greek tragedy. It achieves, in fact, that rarity: a true catharsis.

Ebbe Neergaard mentions that in order to obtain the many low-angled shots he wanted, Dreyer had holes dug all over the set for the camera to be placed in. This caused some amusement among the company, who changed Dreyer's name to Gruyère, on account of the cheesy look of the set. More aptly, Paul La Cour, Dreyer's assistant, said that they made the film on their knees. "It is," Neergaard comments, "a film made kneeling, and this shines out of its style."

A year or two later *St. Joan the Maid* was directed by Marco de Gastybe, with Simone Genevois, and in 1935 U.F.A. produced a German version, *Joan the Maid*, directed by Gustaf Ucicky. According to contemporary criticism, this is a baffled and by no means bright Joan, doing her best for her country but without knowing how her efforts will be used, and becoming the political puppet of the Dauphin. The spiritual aspect is played down. Angela Salloker is praised for her performance of Joan as the perfect patriot, but the emphasis is shifted to Charles VII and on the whole Joan herself can make only a minor impression.

In 1949 came a "big" production, Victor Fleming's *Joan of Arc*, starring Ingrid Bergman. This is based on a play by Maxwell Anderson, but the intellectual content has been thrown over for "dramatic highlights," with pretty, sincere Ingrid striding and riding tomboyishly about in sumptuously shining armour, banners flying, battles clashing, and much flamboyant box-office pageantry. Miss Bergman played St. Joan again in 1954, in a film directed by Roberto Rossellini entitled *Joan of Arc at the Stake* and based on the oratorio by the Swiss composer Arthur Honegger.

In 1953 Jean Delannoy made a three-part film entitled *Destinées* (English translation of this title—*Love, Soldiers and Women!*) Joan appears in the first episode. She is seen trying to enlist soldiers for her cause, and while thus engaged is summoned to baptise a dying baby. The child recovers, and the peasants declare that a miracle has been wrought. The baby at once dies, Joan hears voices telling of her capture and death, and rides off with her troupe. The authors of this oddity

Right, box office pageantry: Ingrid Bergman's ST. JOAN
Below, Shavian dialectic: Richard Widmark and Jean Seberg in Preminger's production of Bernard Shaw's ST. JOAN

The sober truth of Florence Carrez's Joan. . . .

are Jean Aurenche and Pierre Bost, and Joan is played by Michèle Morgan.

Otto Preminger's *Saint Joan* (1957) is derived from Bernard Shaw's play and scripted with great ingenuity and care by Graham Greene. Preminger has been criticised for casting the entirely inexperienced Jean Seberg as Joan, but all in all she manages surprisingly well in conveying as much as she does of the essential loneliness and ultimate agony of the "real" Joan. Shaw's depiction of the Maid, however, has not very much depth. For instance: the true climax of Joan's

122

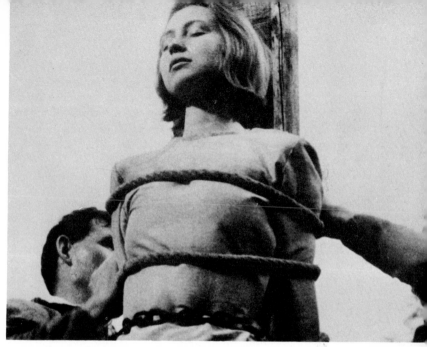

.... *Bresson's TRIAL OF JOAN OF ARC*

life is her recantation—Shaw's Joan recants for the totally ma-
terialistic and egoistic reason that she doesn't like the idea of
imprisonment, dashing to the table and tearing up her paper
like any bad-tempered hoydenish sixth-former. (Compare the
shattering spiritual desolation of Falconetti in her lonely cell.)
If the later characterisation is a failure, the fault may be
Shaw's as much as Seberg's.

For his *Trial of Joan of Arc* (1962) Robert Bresson went
back to the actual minutes of the Court. Even for Bresson,
the treatment is sober. Nothing of any consequence has been

added to the actual records, though these have, of course, been subject to editing and selection. It differs from all other Joan films in being a record rather than an interpretation. The difference between Bresson and Dreyer is indicated in the titles. The Trial—The Passion. Bresson places before us the Trial as it was—not with an attempt at historical reconstruction but, rather, in essence. The camera is used as a recording instrument, neither commenting nor dramatising, repeating over and over again the same angled shots—Joan, her judges, the cell, the watchers, the monk anxious to help and warn—unvaryingly following the question-and-answer rhythm of the Trial. In an interesting interview (*Movie*, number 7), Bresson states that for him the Trial is a duel between Bishop Cauchon and Joan, with the English and the priests functioning as witnesses only. He also says that he expects the audience to bring to the film "not their brains but their capacity for feeling." Despite the fact that the sense of conflict is to some extent missing (largely because of Joan's quiet certitude of her ultimate salvation—the calm of the true mystic), Bresson's expectation is reasonable. Far from resulting in monotony, the cool, *ascetic* (an inevitable Bressonian key-word) approach becomes strangely disturbing, drawing the spectator finally into a state of complete involvement—an emotional experience as disturbing as, and hardly less intense than, that of Dreyer's masterpiece. Added to this is the plain fascination of seeing what we know to be a closer approximation to the actual details than is afforded by any other version. Florence Carrez's composed, externalised, yet deeply affecting Joan is exactly suited to the mood of this wonderful film.

Several early films on St. Francis appeared from Italy. Enrico Guazzoni directed one in 1911, and in 1918 Emilio Ghione brought out *The Pilgrim* and Mario Corsi *Brother Sun*, in the latter of which Umberto Palmarini played the Saint.

Extant stills indicate that *The Pilgrim* was a highly melodramatic affair—in one a group of posturing, bobbed-haired courtiers surround a bishop with heaven-raised eyes clasping to his bosom an equally bobbed-haired, but loin-clothed St. Francis. A photograph of Palmarini in *Brother Sun*, by contrast, is of considerable beauty and dignity.

Also from Italy came Giulio Antamaro's *The Passion of St. Francis,* with Alberto Pasquali (1933), and from Mexico a *St. Francis of Assisi* directed by Tito Gout and produced by Pedro A. Calderon (*c.* 1943). Calderon was also responsible for films on the lives of St. Juan Bosco and St. Antonio di Padua. Jose Luis Jiminez plays Francis and the film, presented at the Locarno International Film Festival, was immensely successful in its country of origin.

In 1951 Roberto Rossellini made *St. Francis, Jester of God.* The script was taken from episodes in *The Little Flowers of St. Francis* (the film is also known as *The Flowers of St. Francis*) and contains stories of Brother Ginepro, Brother Fiore and Sister Chara, treated as though to provide illustrations to a text with which an audience would already be familiar. Criticisms of the film vary from "a courage and validity of intentions well out of the ordinary" to "no attempt to present St. Francis in the round" and "lack of form."

The American *Francis of Assisi* (1960, *dir.* Michael Curtiz), has the special interest of actual locations. Apparently the director, after considerable pondering as to which district was most likely to resemble Assisi, had the happy idea that it might be Assisi itself. The churches of San Pietro and San Damiano were used in Assisi, and, in Perugia, Sant' Angelo. The result is a pictorially exquisite film—reverent, modest, unsensational, and a little dull. It suffers from a few unfortunate lines of dialogue ("I'm off to the Crusades!") and conveys little of religious fervour, but its lack of bloated spectacle and its factual approach go far towards compensating for a certain flatness of treatment.

Henry King, who in 1924 directed Lillian Gish in *The White Sister*, is also responsible for *The Song of Bernadette* (1943). This tells the famous story of Bernadette Soubirous, the daughter of a poor labourer, who has a vision of "the Lady" one day while out collecting firewood. She is told to dig in the sand at a certain spot, does so, and a spring flows out. From this miracle arises the great Catholic shrine of Lourdes. As with *Monsieur Vincent*, it may have been some deep yearning for spiritual refreshment during the gloom of the war years which gave this film its highly enthusiastic reception, because in fact it is handled in typical "Hollywood-religious" manner, all stops (and particularly *vox humana*) full out. The result is sentimental and superficial. Jennifer Jones, in 1943 a newcomer, is simple, pretty, screws up her eyes nicely and looks suitably awed when cued. But she is surely far too healthy and well-fed for the sickly, visionary daughter of a poverty-stricken family. Other characterisations are equally conventional, and Gladys Cooper tends to overplay as a "jealous nun." Once again, visual beauty (the whole thing is stunningly photographed) is no substitute for emotional depth, and there is little sense of mystery or "revelation." The scenario is based on a very sentimentalised best-selling novel and this is, perhaps, a pity.

A more serious study of St. Bernadette is the 1960 French-Italian production *Il suffit d'aimer* (*Bernadette of Lourdes*) directed by Robert Darène, a large part of which deals with her convent life after the miracle. Danièle Ajoret's portrayal is beautiful throughout. The "vision" is seen only through the girl's reaction to it—a reticence as telling here as, at the other end of the scale, the unseen as against the visible menace in a thriller.

126

A film of the actual pilgrimage to Lourdes was made as early as 1903 by Gaumont (*Pèlerinage national à Lourdes*), and Pathé brought out another in the same year which was charmingly described as "reconstructed, with a miracle." Lourdes is also the subject of a film by Julien Duvivier made in 1924 and entitled *The Miracle of Lourdes*, alternatively *The Tragedy of Lourdes*. This was intended as the first part of a controversial trilogy on the subject of the clash between science and religion. The second part, *The Agony of Jerusalem*, appeared in 1926, but the third, *Jesus the Humanitarian*, was never completed. Two short documentaries may also be noted: *Lourdes and Its Miracles* (1954) written and directed by Georges Rouquier, who also spoke the commentary, and *Lourdes* (1966, *dir*. Christian Gion). The former is in three parts—(a) mainly medical in approach, interviews with "cured" pilgrims, visits to the Medical Board, etc., (b) tracing the passing of a day in Lourdes during a pilgrimage, (c) dealing with a number of cures—subtitled *The Unexpected*. Rouquier's approach is entirely documentary, putting forward no viewpoint, presenting facts and leaving their interpretation to each viewer. The second film has much the same treatment, without even the addition of a narrator, comment being left to the camera. It opens with the arrival of ailing and crippled pilgrims by plane and train, accompanied by doctors, nursing sisters and singing nuns. As we follow their progress, everything is coolly, dispassionately recorded, from the streets crammed with gimcrack "novelties," cuckoo-clocks, plaster statuettes, music boxes, all looking like one huge garish bazaar—to the solemnity and splendour of impressive ceremony, the business-like bustle and boundless compassion of those ministering to the invalids, the torchlight processions, the crutch-festooned Grotto, the pain and faith and clatter and nobility and cheapness and grandeur—the hope and the helplessness, the absence of peace. It is a film impossible to witness without tears, and in some instances—such as the agonising, interminable efforts to coax the Communion wafer between the dribbling lips of a helpless, unaware child—almost unbearable. Exactly what final impressions the film will leave must obviously depend on the preconceptions of the individual spectator. It may well be one of dismay at the nature of a God who permits such suffering—or of wonder at the strength of the pilgrims' faith rather than admiration for the belief which arouses it—or even of a wry smile at so well-conducted and thriving a business. But the film emphasises none of these. It merely presents—and is unforgettable.

The Gate of Heaven (1944, *dir*. Vittorio De Sica) is an episodic film dealing with the fortunes of a party of afflicted pilgrims who visit the Loreto Shrine. Although it does not penetrate very deeply into the significance of its subject, it is handled with the sober integrity and attention to detail which might be expected from its director, and is interesting in being the start of his association with Cesare Zavattini, who had a share in writing the script.

Three Mexican films dealing with the legend of the Virgin of Guadalupe may be mentioned here. The Festival is founded on a tale of the days of the Conquistadors, when a poor Indian, Juan Diego, became a Christian after receiving a vision of the Virgin Mary at Tepeyac. The first film, *La Reina da Mexico,* is a plain documentary of the ceremony. Ramon Novarro appeared in the second, *La Virgin Que Forjo Una Patria.* Dates of these two are difficult to ascertain, but appear to be in the early Forties. The third film, *La Virgin Morena* (*The Virgin of Guadalupe*) seems to be the only one widely shown outside its country of origin. The date of release was 1943, and the director Gabriel Soria. It incorporates fictional elements into the legend, with restraint however, and has the actor Jose Luis Jiminez, already mentioned in connection with *St. Francis of Assisi,* as the convert Juan Diego.

An American production, *The Miracle of Fatima* (1952, *dir.* John Brahm) concerns yet another vision of the Virgin Mary, as she appeared to three children in a Portuguese village in 1917. Despite official religious antipathy, and the reluctance of the Church, their story spreads. Eventually miracles occur —afflicted people are healed, the sun appears to lurch downwards to the earth. Notwithstanding such excitements, the general effect is uninspired. Matters are not helped by some crude anti-Russian propaganda: this was perhaps inevitable when the date of production is noted, but that the Virgin Mary should have used three Portuguese village children to warn the world to watch out for trouble from Moscow (the warning remaining unrecorded until conveniently to hand thirty-five years later), seems—let us say—improbable. The entire account of this shrine, in fact, was twisted to provide the dramatics inseparable from the attempt to exploit a religious story. A feature-length documentary dealing with the *Pilgrimage to Fatima* was made by Andrew Buchanan in 1949, scripted by the Rev. John A. V. Burke. The finance was contributed by the readers of the Catholic newspaper *Universe—* thus paralleling *Monsieur Vincent.* It is interesting to note that Buchanan, a Quaker, gave his services and studio facilities for the making of this film.

Our last film concerned with miracles of the Virgin Mary is wholly captivating—an animated cartoon by Paul Terry entitled *The Juggler of Our Lady* (1957), illustrating the famous legend of the humble juggler who, disappointed in his hopes of reforming the world by his art, enters a monastery. There he is looked down upon because he has nothing to offer to Mary but his one ability. On the great Feast Day, however, she favours his juggling above all other gifts.

The film, shot in Cinemascope with stylised drawings, has a beautifully spoken commentary by Boris Karloff.

A famous "miracle" film of its day was *The Miracle of the Wolves* (1924, *dir.* Raymond Bernard), set in the reign of Louis XI and made in Carcassonne. It is an enormous historical spectacle, introducing among its scenes of siege and capture the old legend of the wolves who crouched down in reverence before a young girl kneeling in prayer. *The Sky over the Marshes* (*Cielo Sulla Palude* 1949, *dir.* Augusto Genina) tells of Maria Goretti, a girl of twelve who was murdered in 1902 by a farm labourer whose sexual suggestions and assaults she had resisted. As a result of her extraordinarily positive cultivation of the virtue of chastity she was canonised some fifty years later. (Capital punishment was not legal in Italy, and her murderer, Alessandro, lived to repent and was present at her canonisation.) Set very beautifully against the wide landscapes of the Pontine Marshes, the film is notable for its quiet integrity, neither sentimentalising nor dramatising the events it recreates.

Rossellini's *The Miracle* (1950) originally formed the second half of a two-part film conceived as a sort of concerto for Anna Magnani. In it she plays a half-witted peasant woman who is seduced one day by a passing stranger on the hillside where she is minding her flocks. She becomes pregnant, is convinced that her assailant was St. Joseph, and announces that a miracle has occurred—she is carrying the Messiah. Mocked by the villagers, she staggers away to bear her child in an empty church. Though Miss Magnani's performance is commended, the film as a whole has received severe criticism. For one thing, it is pointed out, no Italian peasants would treat pregnancy, however incurred, with such cruelty and scorn. But the film probably suffers from lacking its first part.

In *Marcelino* (1955, *dir.* Ladislao Vajda), a monk tells a sick child about the figure of Christ on his Cross in a monastery, befriending a little boy who in pity brings him bread and wine. These he takes from the storeroom. The monks, who had originally taken the little boy in when he was found crouching by their gate, trace the cause of the pilfering. The Figure, however, has that day promised to grant the boy his dearest wish—to see his mother, and when the monks find him he is lying smiling happily, by the foot of his Friend. The film had a considerable success and is described by one eminent French critic as "stupefying."

An odd little film is the American *Miracle in the Rain* (1956), directed by Rudolph Maté from a script by Ben Hecht, concerning a lonely New York typist whose one love affair, with a cheerful, kind-hearted soldier, is abruptly terminated when he is posted overseas and killed in action. Every day she seeks comfort in prayer at St. Patrick's Cathedral. She becomes ill but, half-delirious, stubbornly makes her way to the Cathedral in the pouring rain, where she imagines she sees her lover on the steps outside. He tells her they will not be alone any more. In her vision, he returns to her an old coin she had given him as a keepsake. She collapses on the steps, and a priest finds her and carries her inside to shelter. The coin is found grasped in her hand. This simple and potentially embarrassing little story is saved from over-sentimentality by a most moving performance from Jane Wyman, and the general unassuming tenderness of the direction. It is shot largely on location, and is an early example of the modern use of the hidden camera.

Ingmar Bergman's *The Virgin Spring* (1959) concerns another miraculous flow of water but, as might be expected, the circumstances of its uprising are very different from those of the films discussed earlier. Here is no beatific vision, but

131

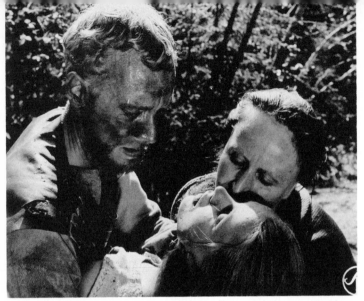

THE VIRGIN SPRING: the murdered daughter
(Max von Sydow as the father)

the brutal rape and murder of a spoilt and arrogant girl who by her attitude half invites the assault. The girl's father avenges her death on the herdsmen who caused it, with even greater cruelty than they had been guilty of themselves. Thereafter he regrets his actions and, together with his wife, goes to seek his daughter's body. As they raise it from the ground, a spring gushes out from the spot on which it had been lying. The story, based on an old legend, has all the symbolism, undertones, ambivalence and strange supplementary characters to be found in any Bergman film. Karin, the girl, is accompanied on her ride through the woods by her half-sister—vicious, jealous, illegitimately pregnant, who hides a toad in one of the loaves of bread they take on their journey; there are hints of incest in the father-daughter relationship, and of jealousy on the part of the mother; the body of one of the murderers, though it would seem that he thoroughly deserves his fate, is left by chance in the position of a man crucified. Once again Bergman's subject is the opposition of good and evil, but elaborated and thickened in typical fashion by doubt, by underlying themes of expiation, self-knowledge,

THE VIRGIN SPRING
Karin, the vicious half-sister
(Gunnel Lindblom)

THE VIRGIN SPRING

evil purged by catastrophe, the eternal human paradox, the unanswered question. But, as Peter Cowie remarks at the end of his full analysis of the film (in *Swedish Cinema*)—"The appearance of the spring is a wonderfully positive gesture. 'The person in the dark' has replied."

Thomas More was canonised by Pope Pius XI in 1935. *A Man for All Seasons* (1966, *dir.* Fred Zinnemann, and scripted from his own play by Robert Bolt, a non-Catholic) concerns itself almost solely with the events mainly responsible for this—his stand against Henry VIII's demand for a divorce in order to marry Anne Boleyn—and this results in a rather two-dimensional, whitewashed portrait of this colourful, complex man. By excluding his less admirable attributes it deprives him to some extent of his humanity, and consequently

*An admirable
performance:
Paul Scofield as
Thomas More in
A MAN FOR ALL SEASONS*

lessens his interest as a character. Paul Scofield as More does full justice to the script, and invests the character with a quiet dignity, humour, and resignation which do not conceal the iron purpose beneath. He brings out admirably any man's natural love of life, and reluctance to keep to the resolve which will deprive him of it. His final parting from his family in the cell is very moving, and here the human agony of his dilemma is presented with heart-rending clarity.

8. Allegories, Parables, Mysticism

JEROME K. JEROME's famous parabolic play *The Passing of the Third Floor Back*, an Edwardian morality, was first produced in the theatre in 1908. An early film version appeared in 1917, directed by Herbert Brenon, in which Sir Johnston Forbes-Robertson repeated on the screen the part he had created on the stage of the mysterious Stranger who comes into a middle-class London boarding-house and sets to rights all the problems and troubles of the inmates. As he finally leaves the house, watched by the little servant-girl he has befriended, the shadow of the transom casts the sign of a cross over the door. The idea, of course, creaks nowadays, and has been imitated *ad nauseam* since the play first appeared. Its simple morality, and its faith in the fundamental goodness of humanity are out of date (not necessarily a matter on which we can congratulate ourselves), but in its day it seemed profound and true—and it made a lot of money. It is difficult to see how so wordy a play could have been transformed for the screen without a stupefying flood of captions, but Forbes-Robertson received high praise for his performance. He himself is reported to have ended by loathing the role in the theatre, and to have come off-stage each night uttering very un-Stranger-like epithets.

The 1935 dialogue version (*dir.* Berthold Viertel) lacks Forbes-Robertson's great presence, and the casting of Conrad Veidt in his place is odd. However, there are some quite strong scenes of the confrontation of good and evil (the latter represented mainly by Frank Cellier)—with, as so often happens, evil seeming the most interesting. The film is notable for the touching performance by Rene Ray as the little servant. Her scenes with the Stranger are illuminated by a Christ-like glow of compassion.

136

Moby Dick, Herman Melville's tremendous allegory of evil and demoniac possession, was emasculated in both John Barrymore versions (*The Sea Beast*, 1926, *dir.* Millard Webb; *Moby Dick*, 1930, *dir.* Lloyd Bacon), to accompany a sultry love story (find the woman in Melville), plus a happy ending after some exciting work with the harpoons. The publicity for the first version reads: "Though a license, it is a relief and a satisfaction that the picture version allows Ahab to live—with a mind restored and with some of earth's possessions and happiness. There is in this interpretation a kind of justice which satisfies rudimentary humaneness and compassion"! The pity is that in Barrymore's performance, particularly in the silent film, there are glimpses of the great Ahab he might have been, and apparently wanted to be, but for the wisdom of the bosses.

John Huston's version (1956) avoids such travesty and, though concentrating to a certain extent on spectacle and external excitement, does afford glimpses of the grandeur of Melville. The enthusiasm, care and understanding which went into its making are still obvious throughout. Gregory Peck's Ahab was not too kindly received by some critics, but his task was a well-nigh insuperable one, and he brought to it a considerable power and presence which deserved a better recognition. Orson Welles has a tremendous few minutes as Father Mapple. The "layers of meaning" which enwrap the symbolism of the white whale are probably impossible to capture in visual terms, and Rod Steiger's radio version, appealing to the illimitable regions of the mind's eye, comes nearest to conveying the immensity and terror of the book.

Melville's other great allegory of good and evil, *Billy Budd*, also proves somewhat intractable film material, though Peter Ustinov's 1962 production is by no means unsuccessful. The symbolism, perhaps, is less complex than that of *Moby Dick*, but the mere fact of watching the story performed by actors

137

A fine and complex study: Robert Ryan as the villainous Claggart in BILLY BUDD

reduces the theme from the general to the particular. Robert Ryan's Claggart, for instance, though a fine and complex study of villainy, is not, and could not be, the dark personification of evil which Melville suggests. The result is a moving story of betrayal and justice miscarried, rather than a monumental mystical conflict. *Billy Budd,* in fact, needs music such as Benjamin Britten gives it in his opera if it is to be presented on stage or screen and still preserve its larger significance. It

138

requires less realistic treatment than it receives in this often impressive film.

In Bergman's *The Seventh Seal* (1957), the struggle is against Death; not the kindly death that releases from the burden of life, but rather the ultimate and final annihilation. In fact, the Knight who opposes Death over a game of chess gives the impression of being a power of Light against a power of Darkness, and the fact that he "saves" from his opponent a little family of strolling players—obviously symbolising the Holy Family—strengthens this suggestion. The action takes place in the Middle Ages—plague-ridden, superstitious, cruel, ignorant, where life is "nasty, brutish and short." In the midst of witch-burning, religious flagellation, thieving, murder and disease, the Knight plays his game, a game he and all with him must lose in the end. The Knight seeks only to postpone this end so that before it comes he can prove himself and resolve his own doubts. In the closing moments he and those he has met on his journey are being led across the skyline in the Dance of Death. The little family remain. This is, of course, an extreme simplification of both the story and the significance of the complex and beautiful film—about which an immense amount has already been written. It is no naïve parable on the triumph of "simple faith." Bergman indicates that man loses his freedom of action if he comes under the influence of the Church, which is shown in all its mediaeval grimness and dark power, and the "Holy Family" are travelling artists. The verse in the Book of Revelations from which the title is taken is quoted at the start of the film: "And when he had opened the seventh seal, there was silence in heaven about the space of half an hour"—surely one of the most terrifying verses in the whole book.

Three more of Bergman's tormented struggles towards, or with, God, may be briefly mentioned here: briefly, because

detailed analyses of any would demand far more space than is available and are already to be found in many studies, notably Peter Cowie's *Swedish Cinema*. In addition, the scripts themselves have been published in English translation.

Through a Glass Darkly is the first of a trilogy, the middle film of which is *Winter Light*, referred to previously. This also deals, in part, with a man who has withdrawn (but symbolically) into the world of success. He is a writer of fiction. Bergman here is concerned with what might be vaguely called the love of God, but equally with loneliness, with separation, both of spirit and body. There are only four characters—no-one else is seen at all. The man's son, seventeen, feels neglected by his father and is tormented by his own developing puberty;

Left, top: the Middle Ages—THE SEVENTH SEAL
Left, below: the Dance of Death—THE SEVENTH SEAL
This page: the schizophrenic Karin in
THROUGH A GLASS DARKLY

the daughter Karin is a schizophrenic, solitary in her distorted world where she listens to her private voices—creeping up to an attic room and communing with God through the cracks in the wall-paper; Karin's husband, ineffectual in his efforts to aid his afflicted wife, retreats into his private world of work. After events which culminate in Karin seducing her brother and being taken away to hospital (in a helicopter which, as she sees its approach, causes her to cry out—in a horrifying scene—that God is a spider) a gleam of hope appears that some contact may be made between father and son. His daughter's collapse has shaken the older man into an awareness of his own selfish withdrawal. "God is love," he tells the boy, " . . . *Every* sort of love. The highest and the lowest, the poorest and the richest, the most ridiculous and the most sublime." His hopes, he says, lie in the knowledge that love exists as something real. We cannot know whether love proves God's existence or whether love itself is God. "After all, it doesn't make very much difference." "Daddy spoke to me!" are the boy's final words.

In *The Silence* (1962) there is no mention of God at all—and the very negation hangs heavily over the entire film. (Peter Cowie suggests that He might be symbolised in the army tank which rumbles menacingly and with apparent meaninglessness through the streets of the strange town.) This story of two tormented women, one of them dying from a lung ailment, stranded for a night in a foreign city on their way home from a holiday—a place where neither they nor we understand the language—is among the most despairing and difficult of all Bergman's films. Again there is that universal and all-pervasive theme of the times, failure of communication, this time quite literally, of language itself. Ironically, an age in which the means of communication, from supersonic planes to Telstar, have never progressed with such rapidity or comprehensive-

142

ness, sees the communicators no nearer to (indeed, further from) true communion. The sub-title in the printed script of this film reads, "God's silence—the negative impression"— the theme of the three together is described as, in the metaphysical sense, "a reduction."

The same director's *Wild Strawberries* deals again with the subject of withdrawal. An old scholar, on a journey from his home to a university town where he is to receive an honorary degree, encounters a series of events which, in combination with a terrifying nightmare the evening before, bring him to the realisation of the selfishness of his enclosed existence. Past and present are interwoven in the experiences of this one day. Then, as he lies in bed at its close, a beautiful final vision of his parents, young and happy, waving across the river to him in love and reconciliation, sends him to sleep in peace.

Death is personified in the early Fritz Lang film *Destiny* (1921). The English title is misleading, the literal translation of the original being *The Tired Death* (*Der müde Tod*), which is much more apposite. The French title of *Les Trois Lumières* moves even further away from the central theme. A young girl pleads with Death for her lover's life. He shows her an immense room filled with burning candles, each of which represents a human soul, and says that if she can save any one of three from being extinguished, he will spare her lover. The young couple are taken through three visionary episodes—in Baghdad, Venice and a magical China. In each of them her lover is threatened, in each the girl fails to save him. Afterwards Death, tired of death, offers her a last chance. If she can provide Him with another life, he will spare her lover's. She appeals to a beggar, goes to a home for aged and ailing women. All indignantly refuse to relinquish their presumably miserable lives. There is a fire, and a baby is left behind by the fleeing inmates. The girl rescues it. Death holds out his hands to take this life, but the girl suddenly rebels and saves the child. Death takes the now dying girl to the body of her lover and they are transported up a high mountain. There is much heavy German symbolism of the period, and the three large interpolated spectacles are somewhat diffuse, but even now the film has a strange fascination and power, particularly in such shots as the huge unbroken wall filling the entire screen and dwarfing the tiny human figures at its foot, and the multi-angled array of huge guttering "soul" candles in the dark hall. The last part of the film, with the girl seeking a substitute for death, is the most interesting.

Death's wagon driver appears in the mystical Swedish production *The Phantom Carriage* (or *Thy Soul Shall Bear Witness*, 1920, *dir.* Victor Sjöström) in which a drunkard's soul is taken by the emissary to witness the unhappiness caused by his dissolute life. Salvation Army workers are introduced into the story, which is really a stern sermon of the "Repent ye, for the day cometh . . . " category.

The region traversed between death and the soul's ultimate destination is the setting for the allegorical *Outward Bound* (1931, *dir.* Robert Milton), which is based on Sutton Vane's well-known play of the same title. The district is here represented as a ship whose passengers gradually realise that they have recently died and are "outward bound." As the end of their journey draws near an Examiner arrives and puts them through a sort of Heavenly Board questionnaire. The play's original production caused something of a sensation, and though seeming mild enough now, still has its effective moments—in the scenes of the suicide-pact lovers who are able to return, and the character of the little steward. The direction, very much that of a staged play in photographs, is by later standards inevitably slow and stilted. In the 1944 re-make (*Between Two Worlds, dir.* Edward A. Blatt) the action is moved forward to the Second World War and the catastrophe caused by a bomb explosion, but the somewhat tenuous dramatic effect does not survive this transposition.

The main theme of *Our Town* (1940), Sam Wood's film version of Thornton Wilder's very beautiful play, is that happiness should be experienced more consciously while it so briefly lasts. In the last section a young woman, one of the inhabitants of the little American town Grover's Corner, is lying dangerously ill on her second child-bed. She foresees her own death and, in the light of this prescience, is given the opportunity of re-visiting her own youth. She chooses her sixteenth birthday, when she, her family, and the young man who became her husband, went off for a summer picnic. Poignantly she watches them all as they bustle about, careless and carefree, unwittingly moving through her, unheeding the flashing past of time. "Just look at me *one minute* as though you really saw me!" she pleads to her mother. The whole existence of Grover's Corner passes before us during the course of the film, commented on by the kindly, humorous, tolerant and at times slightly acid figure of the local drug-store keeper —replacing the Stage Manager of the play. Above, from the hill-top cemetery, the dead of the little town watch, calm and remote, "waitin' for somethin' they all feel is comin'—somethin' important and great. Aren't they waitin' for the eternal part in them to come out clear?" "The dead," remarks the commentator, "don't stay interested in us livin' people for very long. Gradually, gradually, they lose hold of the earth, and the people they loved. They stay here while the earth part of them burns away, burns out, and all that time they slowly get indifferent to what's goin' on in Grover's Corner." The young woman joins them, and is quietly welcomed. "I didn't *realise*," she says. "All that was going on and we never *noticed.*" The young man visits the cemetery and flings himself down by her grave in an agony of grief. "Goodness!" says one of the women, "that ain't no way to behave." "They don't understand, do they?" the girl says. "No—they don't understand." The film is a fantasy of the most exquisite tenderness and humanity—moving yet never sentimental, compassionate yet never depressing—often, in fact, extremely amusing—and with a theme as relevant today as yesterday, and tomorrow. It should certainly have a place in the cinema repertoire.

In *The Road to Heaven* (1942, *dir.* Alf Sjöberg) the ultimate destination of the good is literally the Elysian Fields, filled with flowers. Critically acclaimed as an important landmark in the resurgence of the Swedish cinema, it is a sort of Pilgrim's Progress towards the Green Pastures—Mats setting off on his journey after his *fiancée* has been unjustifiably burnt as a witch. *En route* he is tempted by the Devil, and succumbs to lead a life of greed and dissipation. On his deathbed, after fruitless attempts at self-justification, he is forgiven by the Good Father who has watched over him from the beginning.

Heaven appears again in the English *A Matter of Life and Death* (1946, *dir.* Michael Powell and Emeric Pressburger), and appears to resemble a sort of immense sports arena. The story concerns an injured airman who, while undergoing a brain operation, has delusions that he is being tried by a Celestial Court composed of famous historical characters. They have ruled that he should have died on a certain date, but failed to do so owing to a heavenly clerical error. He is now summoned to plead for his continued existence. The treatment is witty and original, with strikingly original settings and effects and much of the Powell-Pressburger panache which, despite its occasional pretentiousness, was a necessary and saving stimulant in the drab days when it first appeared. Unfortunately, the Court proceedings develop into a sort of Anglo-American wrangle, and the more this is expanded the more its interest evaporates. Even so, the film hardly deserves the ten full pages of virulent, hysterical abuse flung at it by the Robsons in their book *The World Is My Cinema*.

Death in Cocteau's *Orphée* (1950) is a beautiful young Princess who goes about in a large car; her harbingers are motor-cycle riders, helmeted and goggled. The "shades," entered through a dissolving mirror, are the shadowy ruins of St. Cyr. Life and death, in this modern fable of Eurydice, are ruled by a voice on the radio speaking an apparently non-sensical code, the Bacchantes a group of art students, Judgment is delivered by civil-service type questioners in a shabby underground room. The radio is also used for supernatural messages in *The Next Voice You Hear* (1950. *dir*. William A. Wellman), but this time by God Himself. A typical American family, in a typical American small town, with typical family problems, are listening to the radio. Suddenly the programme fades out and a strange voice is heard from the speaker: "This is God. I will be with you for the next few days." They think it is some kind of hoax, but the same words have been heard simultaneously all over the world—in each country in its own language. Sincere and reticent (the Voice, for example, is never actually heard, only reported), the film is considerably less naïve and glib than may appear from this bald account of its opening sequence. However, the Almighty spends a disproportionate time in solving this one family's affairs, and these do not really match their intended symbolic counterparts in the world as a whole. God really finds everything a bit too uncomplicated. Cling to the good old American virtues, His ruling seems to be, and everything will be okay. To others, however, it may seem that He is very easily satisfied.

Adult religious hypocrisy and bigotry are contrasted with the innocent liturgical games of children in René Clément's *Jeux Interdits* (1952). A little girl whose parents and pet dog have been killed during the fall of France is found by a young farm boy and taken to his home, where she is given shelter. She has heard that people are buried in cemeteries so as not to be alone, and wants this for her puppy, with real crosses. The little boy promises to do this for her, and buries the dog together with other dead animals. At his uncle's funeral, the children are unable to take their eyes off the numerous crosses; afterwards the boy steals a barrowload to furnish the "cemetery." Horrified at the desecration of the churchyard, his family accuse the neighbours. A furious row builds up, culminating in a wild fight between the men, who fall into a newly dug grave. Completely detached, the children watch. The little girl's eyes are fixed on yet another cross. embroidered on the stole of the horrified priest. Eventually the boy's secret activities are discovered. The girl is to be sent away, never having seen the animal cemetery. The boy promises to reveal where he has put the crosses if she is allowed to stay. The father agrees, then breaks his word, and the boy, heartbroken, hurls the crosses into the river. The little girl is taken to the crowded railway station. Left alone for a moment, she thinks she sees her erstwhile friend in the crush, runs from the place she has been told to stay in, and is once again alone and lost.

The betrayal of innocence, though of an adult, is also the motive in the remarkable Brazilian film *The Given Word* (1961, *dir.* Anselmo Duarte). The story is simple and straightforward. A peasant has made a vow that if his injured donkey, vital to the livelihood of himself and his wife, recovers from an accident, he himself will carry a full-sized cross thirty miles to the church in Salvador as a token of thanksgiving.

148

The donkey does recover and, with simple integrity, the peasant and his wife set out. But the vow which Ze, the peasant, made was to Iansam, the goddess of thunder and lightning held by the countryfolk to be the pagan equivalent to the Catholic Santa Barbara. The priest, Father Olavo, harshly denies Ze entrance to the church. Ze's wife tries to persuade him to leave, but he is stubborn in his determination to fulfill his vow. Crowds begin to gather; the sense that something is afoot goes through the town; a local reporter, unscrupulous and slick, blows the event up into a political issue, hinting at a subversive motive for the disturbance. Ze's wife, increasingly upset, becomes estranged from him. A local lay-about seduces her and later denounces Ze to the police as an agitator. By this time almost the entire population is milling around in the wildest excitement and the whole affair has turned into a sort of gigantic and dangerous spree. The police come to arrest Ze and, driven beyond endurance, he tries to enter the church by force. In the growing violence and confusion, he is killed by a stray bullet. Ze is lifted on the cross he has brought so far, and the crowd, abashed, carry him into the church. This brief summary, with its inevitable emphasis on some possibly melodramatic elements in the plot, cannot adequately convey the power and atmosphere the film engenders. Merely as a piece of dramatic entertainment it is gripping throughout—from the low-toned start of the journey, through the gradual, beautifully controlled crescendo of din and confusion, frenzied crowds and furious movement, to the final climax and brief coda. Its theatrical origins show only, if at all, in the adherence to one locality for a great part of its length, and the lengthy opening sequence is pure, and admirable, cinema. The main setting of the great church towering arrogantly and formidably above its enormous flight of steps is awesome and magnificent—the symbolism may be

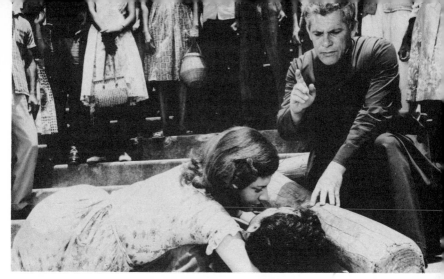

Left, the peasant Ze sets out to keep his vow—the opening of the Brazilian THE GIVEN WORD; and above, Ze's death—the betrayal of innocence

obvious, but it is highly effective, and it is the whole point and intention of the film that it *should* be of crystal clarity. It is, in fact, a modern morality, and at least it has the strength of its commitment. And it is in no way a film of black-and-white naïvete. Ze is no whitewashed plaster saint. He is maddeningly stubborn, ruthless to his wife, and it is his own loss of temper which, almost literally, triggers off his death. Neither is it, as might appear from the summary, an anti-Catholic film, nor an anti-religious film. It is an anti-bigotry, anti-intolerance film, and is tough and uncompromising in its approach. It is also unforgettably moving.

The Forbidden Christ (1950) is the only film directed by Curzio Malaparte, an Italian journalist who in his time had

151

been connected with both Nazis and Communists. This perhaps accounts for the ambiguous character of the Christ figure in his film—a carpenter who falsely confesses to having betrayed a young Italian partisan to the Nazis, in order to save the boy's brother (his own best friend) from committing further violence in his search for the betrayer. The brother, Bruno, kills the carpenter and then, when the real betrayer confesses, finds himself unable to commit further violence in revenge. In outline it resembles a sacrificial act on the part of the carpenter. However, he is by no means a saintly figure, and the religious-sounding title is equally equivocal. A comparison of English and Italian criticism of the film is interesting—the former finding it a "powerful and sometimes preten-

Procession: FORBIDDEN CHRIST

tious allegory of guilt and expiation" concerning a man "purged of violence by his own violence," and an Italian describing it as having "no true emotion, not a quiver of true humanity." It is based on a true incident.

Balthazar (*Au Hasard Balthazar*, 1966, *dir*. Robert Bresson) is a donkey. Bresson's film tells of its life, suffering and death. When newly born, it is adopted by two children, Jacques and Marie. Thenceforward the animal's life and Marie's touch at intervals, notably when Balthazar escapes from its owner, for whom it has been carting sand, and returns to her when she is a young girl in her 'teens. The donkey is passed from hand to hand and is killed, by a shot from a customs officer, while being used by a gang of smugglers. It dies among a flock of sheep. The last glimpse seen of the girl is of her cowering naked in a corner after being beaten by the smugglers' leader who earlier on had seduced her. The symbolism and Christ-references are fairly obvious throughout, and the film could be taken as a straightforward parable. Bresson, however, is rarely as uncomplicated as his austerity and simplicity of treatment make him appear, and the whole range of human suffering and helplessness is enclosed in the confines of this deceptively detached film.

A parallel may be found in Bresson's later film *Mouchette* (1967), the story of the last few days in the life of a fourteen-year-old peasant girl whose miserable circumstances—a dying mother, callous, drunken father, mocking school fellows, hopeless impossibility of escape—drive her to seek release in death. After a brutal rape by a poacher she had tried to help, and the death of her mother before she could recount what had happened to her, Mouchette wraps herself in a dress given to her by a curtly "sympathetic" neighbour and, after several attempts, rolls down the bank into the river and drowns herself. The deep but cool compassion of the film—made even

153

more poignant by brief glimpses of the happy young girl she *could* have been—lift it well above the merely depressive level, and her death is quite explicitly shown to be something more than a mere "blessed release."

In *Whistle Down the Wind* (1961, *dir.* Bryan Forbes) a bearded man is found hiding in a barn by three local children, two girls and a small boy. Their heads full of Sunday School teaching, and having just had an encounter with the Salvation Army group, they take him to be Jesus Christ. In fact, he is a murderer, and is later cornered by the police. Rather than betray their faith in him (or so it seems, though his motive is never made explicit) he gives himself up, instead of attempting to shoot his way out, and is led away to prison. This potentially sentimental idea is treated with such restraint and robust common sense on the part of the children that embarrassment is avoided almost throughout. The carefully contrived preparation of their state of mind up to the time when they find the man makes their belief in his being Jesus entirely credible, and their matter-of-fact attitude and practical discussions as to how this complicated situation can best be handled are equally touching and humorous. The little boy is saltily sceptical, especially after the man has failed to save his kitten's life. "That's not Jesus—that's just a feller." Later, the news of Christ's second coming spreads to the children around the district, and here belief becomes somewhat strained. The allegorical parallels, too, are more forced, such as the boy who betrays the secret three times under threats from the local bully. The final glimpse of the

Left, top: a child's suicide by drowning—
the closing sequence of Bresson's MOUCHETTE
Below, Christ's second coming? The children
face the Stranger in WHISTLE DOWN THE WIND

man, outlined in cruciform fashion against the sky as the police search him for weapons, has been criticised as a facile *cliché*, but the moment is brief, and what may appear trite in some circumstances can touch the heart in others. The photography catches the bleak beauty of the Northern countryside and, together with the unpretentious direction, down-to-earth performances and Malcolm Arnold's hauntingly atmospheric music, transforms what could have been a very sugary confection into something memorably tender and true.

An altogether more peculiar allegory is *Cool Hand Luke* (1967, *dir*. Stuart Rosenberg), in which Paul Newman plays a sort of Christ-convict. The allegorical significance of the film has not always been noticed, though the pointers are there clearly enough, with the result that the motivation of Luke's character has been regarded as insufficiently brought out. Just what sort of man is he? Why *does* he suffer for the other convicts? An early hint is given in the very pointlessness of the "crime" for which he is arrested and sentenced to the chain gang—he is caught breaking off the tops of parking meters with a wrench during a drunken, lonely spree. The punishment is so far out of proportion to the crime that he immediately becomes a figure of sympathy. The Christ parallels develop slowly. An early shot, after he has fought the bully of the chain gang, shows him cowled with a white towel in a manner unmistakably resembling the conventional Bible picture. The other convicts become his disciples, and later betray him—he is punished for their misdeeds—his mother is brought to see him (in a van, for she is paralysed) and reproaches him for having left her. The extraordinary egg-eating sequence concerns the symbolic source of life, and an act of eating performed as more than the mere consumption of food. At the end of the film Luke, escaping from the camp, finds refuge in a deserted chapel, his Gethsemane, and talks to God. In the course of

156

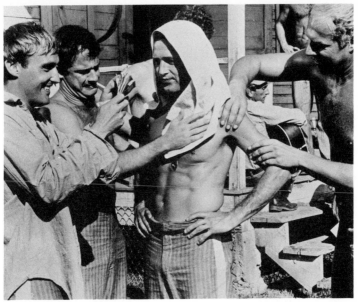

Convict and disciples:
Paul Newman (centre) as COOL HAND LUKE

Luke's capture and death, the mirrored spectacles of the sinister overseer are broken, symbolically foretelling the end of his reign of blind brutality. The purpose and ethics are alike obscure. The maltreated convict-disciples are thieves, or murderers, receiving their due punishments, and it is noticeable that we see or hear nothing of their victims. The film can be taken as a beautifully photographed, powerfully directed prison-thriller, but the religious significance is plain—a parallel with the Christ who dwelt among sinners, who was (in the film's catch-phrase) the "man who will not conform."

9. The Dark Side

THE DEVIL LOST NO TIME in making his way to the cinema screen and *Faust,* with variations, proved the most popular of all legends. Méliès made at least two versions, in 1897 and 1903, and an early English production (1897) was directed by G. A. Smith, the British film pioneer whose strange history is told in some detail in Trevor H. Hall's *Strange Case of Edmund Gurney.* In the first few years of the century numerous further filmings appeared, including a one-reeler with Thomas Santschi (*dir.* Francis Boggs) and *Mephisto and the Maiden,* both from Selig in 1908, and a burlesque from Pathé, *Miss Faust,* in 1909. The first really notable version, however, was the German one directed by F. W. Murnau in 1926. The story was taken from Marlowe, Goethe, and the original German legend. Emil Jannings is a fleshy but flamboyant Mephistopheles in conventional style, all evil leers and towering wickedness. The Marguerite (Camilla Horn) and Faust (Gösta Ekman) are pretty and colourless. The film sacrifices subtlety to spectacle, but has fine photography, and effects, such as the ride, which still impress today. As Wagenknecht points out, the supernatural scenes really seem supernatural and not just the achievement of camera magic.

An early variant on the story came from Germany in *The Student of Prague* (1913, *dir.* Stellan Rye), which combined the legend with a tale of E. T. A. Hoffmann and Poe's *William Wilson.* Mephistopheles appears as a sorcerer, Scapinelli, and the soul of the Faust figure (named Baldwin) is symbolised by his double, which is enticed out of a mirror. The film was re-made (the best version and still enthralling) in 1926 (*dir.* Henrik Galeen), with Conrad Veidt as Baldwin-Faust and Werner Krauss as Scapinelli. A third version made in Vienna under the Nazis in 1936 with Anton Walbrook was turned into a sort of musical and has little interest.

In 1922 Marcel L'Herbier directed *Don Juan and Faust,* recounting an imaginary meeting between the two figures and apparently making much use of symbolism.

In 1926, the year of the Murnau *Faust* and the second *Student of Prague,* America produced the first of many modern variations, *The Sorrows of Satan,* from Marie Corelli's famous and now unreadable novel. It had previously been filmed in England in 1917 with Cecil Humphreys, but it is the American version, directed by D. W. Griffith, which is remembered today, notably for the way in which the Griffith imagination triumphed over the trashy material, creating in parts at least an impressive film. The prologue, showing the fallen angels being ejected from Heaven—is typical of Griffith's Victorianism, but the early part of the actual story, in which the Devil in the guise of a modern Prince tempts a young writer away from the girl who loves him into the arms of a vamp, has considerable atmosphere, aided by an elegant portrayal of Satan by Adolphe Menjou. His first appearance, invisible beneath an enormous shadow which as he advances dwindles down to his own form, is a wonderfully menacing entrance. Noteworthy too is the revelation of the Prince as Devil, again making ingenious, unforced use of a looming shadow, but this time winged. The same novel vaguely forms the basis for one part of Carl Dreyer's four-episode *Leaves from Satan's Book.* Satan appears in four guises—a Pharisee, an Inquisitor, a leading figure in the French Revolution, and a member of the Red Guard.

William Dieterle's *All that Money Can Buy* (1941) is another modern variant, in which Walter Huston appears as a rustically-clothed, cigar-smoking Devil (Mr. Scratch) in a New England folk story. Huston's is a country legend-type devil

159

Walter Huston's
Mr. Scratch of
ALL THAT
MONEY CAN BUY

who, as light relief from purchasing souls for money or desire, causes the occasional ruinous storm, steals food, curdles milk, and in general brings the frustrations to a farming community that are paralleled by the modern urban mischiefs of George Spiggot in *Bedazzled* (referred to below). Paul Muni in *Angel on My Shoulder* (1946, *dir*. Archie Mayo) is a deceased double-crossed racketeer who, finding Hell unpleasantly hot, makes a bargain with Mephistopheles (Claude Rains). He will be permitted to return to earth in the body of a judge he resembles in order to revenge himself on his double-crosser, provided he also, on the Devil's behalf, undoes all the good work the judge has been doing. Better than it sounds, the film is notable

160

for the witty performances of its two leading actors. Yet another updated version of this period is *Alias Nick Beal* (1949, *dir.* John Fallow) in which Faust is an honest District Attorney who is helped by a mysterious figure, Nick Beal (Ray Milland), to clean up the town and defeat his opponents, and eventually to become Governor. He is then blackmailed by Nick Beal, turning nasty, into visiting the Isle of Lost Souls and afterwards into undoing his good work. However, all is made to end happily by the love of a good woman, and the activities of a clergyman. An interesting twist in the film is the Devil's use of *good* to further his evil purposes, rather than preying on the lower instincts such as greed or desire.

An odd mixture from Italy is *Faust and the Devil* (1949, *dir.* Carmine Gallone), in which the scenario is culled from Goethe plus the Gounod and Boito operas, with additional linking dialogue and much camera trick work. A cautious contemporary report describes the result as "not wholly ineffective."

Treated with typical irony, the Faust legend would seem to be a natural—indeed, a supernatural—for René Clair, who undertook what he describes as his "logical" interpretation, in conjunction with scenarist Armand Salacrou, in *La Beauté du Diable*. In an interview (*Sight and Sound*, March 1950) Clair states his wish to detach himself from Goethe and Marlowe and reconstruct the story on logical grounds. His first objection to the popular version is that no-one seems to inquire about the disappearance of the old Professor following his rejuvenation. Clair's Mephistopheles therefore takes on the appearance of old Dr. Faust at a crucial moment, and is welcomed back unsuspectingly by the University. His second complaint is that old Faust's struggle with his own self before accepting the Devil's offer is far too short and facile. As a "highly learned intellectual, probably an atheist driven to seek recourse in black magic by his disbelief in God," Faust should be shaken to the marrow by the Devil's actually appearing, taking it as an inescapable proof of the existence of God. Clair's Faust has never known the joys of youth and love, and doubts the power of Mephistopheles to provide them. As proof, the latter transforms the old Professor into an impecunious young student who falls in love with a gypsy girl, Marguerita, who is in no way like the conventional Faustian heroine. The young man, Henri, soon learns that youth is valueless without money, so Mephistopheles reveals to him the alchemist's secret. Then, having awakened in Henri a taste for luxury and fame, Mephistopheles removes it all at one blow. Henri is, of course, utterly miserable. But Mephistopheles assures him that one stroke of the pen can restore the lot. Who, in such circumstances, could withstand the temptation? In this way, says Clair, the story is founded on a much more reasonable basis. Later Henri, sated with pleasure, repents. He sees in a vision his magical powers producing dreadful weapons of destruction such as the atomic bomb. He defies Mephistopheles, who brings him to ruin by turning the gold back into its original sand, at the same time causing the economic collapse of the country which Faust had enriched. Henri tears up his agreement, joins with the populace in routing the Devil, and leaves with Marguerite in a rather forced happy ending. Certain English reactions—that Faust having signed his contract should have stood by it willy-nilly— were commented on by Clair: "For these islanders, even the Divine Grace itself cannot oppose the obligations of traditional British honesty."

Another modern variant from France is Claude Autant-Lara's *Marguerite de la Nuit* (1955), set in Paris in the Twenties. Dr. Faust, the last descendant of the Faust of 1480, is on his way home from a performance of "Faust" at the Opéra when he meets a drug trafficker, Dr. Léon, in whom he recognises a reincarnation of Mephistopheles. Marguerite is a dancer in a night club, and Dr. Faust signs a pact with the narcotics Devil to bring her true love. He is thereupon rejuvenated to twenty years. (The old and young Faust are played by different actors.) This time, however, things go wrong. Faust's love is insufficient for Marguerite, who dies mourned only by the Devil. In this modern turnabout Mephistopheles (Yves Montand) is considerably more sympathetic than either old Faust (Palau), who is tedious, or young Faust (Jean-François Calvé), who is uninteresting and superficial.

A West German film directed by Peter Gorski in 1960 is a straightforward reproduction of a stage performance of Goethe, and the little-known American *Faust* of 1964 directed by Michael Susman is described as a version of the legend set in a world of magicians.

The interesting Richard Burton-Neville Coghill *Dr. Faustus* (1967) is a more or less straightforward transcription of Marlowe, derived from a stage production by the Oxford Union Dramatic Society with a few interpolated lines from other plays ("Infinite riches in a little room") and a great deal of camera-magic embellishment. It is almost wholly successful, and what *longueurs* and absurdities there are derive mainly from the original author. Admittedly the slow motion lechery ballet is a mistake, and it is doubtful whether anyone could do much with the Emperor's Court. On the whole, however, there is grandeur and awe, and a true sense of tragic doom. Richard Burton, looking very like Dr. Caligari in his black-rimmed spectacles, is magnificent throughout, and never more so than in his dreadful realisation of the loss of God. Elizabeth Taylor appears not only as Helen but also as a kind of series of Helenic transmogrifications, unwarranted by Marlowe but effective all the same. She turns up finally as the demon who with triumphant shrieks drags Faust to his doom—and a minor criticism

*Sorrowing
Mephistopheles:
Andreas Teuber's
compassionate Fallen
Angel of
DOCTOR FAUSTUS*

might be made that the hell to which he is going, all warm glow and Miss Taylor, looks much too exciting to warrant all the fuss. The actual descent is made literally through the floor and is beautifully contrived to make use of the added freedom of the cinema while still retaining the suggestion of the theatre stage. Most memorable is the Mephistopheles. This grave, compassionate Fallen Angel, true to Marlowe's "devil as a monk" and a long way from the usual sharp-bearded, slant-

164

eyebrowed, agile, glittering figure, is played with astonishing authority and depth by a young American philosophy graduate, Andreas Teuber. The final glimpse of his shaven, sorrowing face, unillusioned rather than disillusioned, stained with tears as he watches Faust going to his doom, is extraordinarily moving. His presence throughout, with its implications of illimitable knowledge of evil and apartness from God, and of the unutterable grief in that knowledge, adds very greatly to the film's considerable stature.

From Marlowe to Peter Cook, and still with Faust. In *Bedazzled* (1967, *dir.* Stanley Donen), Cooks plays Mephisto under the pseudonym of George Spiggott, who offers a little employee in a Wimpy Bar (Dudley Moore) seven wishes in exchange for his soul. At the moment of confrontation Moore is on the point of suicide because he is sick of his dull life and his inability to make any progress with a waitress in the Bar. The rest of the film is a series of "wish-episodes" of varying success. They are apt to go on too long (particularly a seemingly endless and obvious take-off of talkative intellectuals), but opportunities are taken to lob a caustic or satirical comment against almost every facet of present-day life and thought. The result is sometimes jejune, sometimes amusing and quite sharply pointed. Hell is located in a seedy night club (reached by a descending lift) where Raquel Welch as a luscious Lilian Lust dominates the personified Deadly Sins: Heaven is a remote country house (reached by an ascending lift into a large meadow) where God's voice reverberates across an enormous conservatory: miraculous transportations occur in Central London: nuns perform initiation ceremonies on trampolines. Peter Cook is quite a striking Devil in his oblong dark glasses and his cloak, and it is amusing to watch him at his minor devilries such as tearing the final pages out of paperback Agatha Christies or squashing bananas in their crates.

The Devil appears, of course, in numerous films other than the Faustian series, Méliès again leading the way in 1899 with *The Devil in the Convent* and *The Merry Frolics of Satan,* which featured dancing girls in Hell. In 1908 both Edison and Biograph presented versions of *The Devil* from the play of the same name in which George Arliss was scoring a big success in New York. Vitagraph went one better with *He Went To See the Devil Play,* concerning a member of the audience at Arliss's theatre who thereafter saw everyone as a Devil including his wife, and to cap this Selig came out with *The Devil, the Servant and the Man* about a man who saw both *The Devil* and another play, combined both in his dreams, and was induced to return to his deserted spouse. This last was actually produced in three different versions during the following six years with the same star, Kathryn Williams, in each—after which the vein, not surprisingly, was considered worked out. Arliss himself appeared in a full-length version of *The Devil* in the early Twenties and gave his usual polished portmanteau performance. Vitagraph portrayed Hell in *Dante's Inferno* (1911), Milano of Italy did so in *Inferno* (1908), and films of the same title appeared from Fox in 1924 (*dir.* Henry Otto) and 1935 (*dir.* Harry Lachman). The last two pictures framed the Dantesque visions in a melodramatic modern story, but the depictions of the nether regions were not unimpressive in a rather balletic fashion, deriving from the Doré illustrations. The white one-piece bathing suits of the lost ladies of 1924 would doubtless be considered excessive today. The modern Hell, as seen in Sartre's *Huis Clos* (1954, *dir.* Jacqueline Audry) is an elegant hotel room with all mod. cons. but no way out, where the wicked are shut up for ever to torment themselves and one another (and, to some extent, us too) with endless philosophising and recriminating over their past misdeeds.

Luigi Maggi's *Satan—or the Drama of Humanity* (1912) is a

spectacular production featuring the work of the Devil in four different periods—the Garden of Eden, the life of Christ, the Middle Ages, and the modern underworld. In the mediaeval story Satan, somewhat belatedly, invents strong drink to bring humanity to ruin. The stories are told consecutively and do not thus presage *Intolerance*, though according to Wagenknecht the atmosphere and feeling bear some resemblance to Griffith's epic. Griffith in *Home Sweet Home* has a vague suggestion of Hell, apparently looking like a burning hillside, from which the composer of the famous song is drawn up to Heaven by Lillian Gish, doubtless feeling this made all the throes of composition worth while.

Murnau's *Satanas* (1919), with a scenario by Robert Wiene, is a three-episode film, Conrad Veidt appearing as Lucifer in ancient Egypt, Borgian Italy and the Russian Revolution. The theme concerns his search to see if he can find one human being capable of deriving good from evil and ensuring his salvation. The film was regarded in general as an extravagant failure but Veidt, as so often, is outstanding. His search, incidentally, is abortive.

Jules Berry in *Les Visiteurs du Soir* (1942, dir. Marcel Carné) is a mediaeval Devil who sends two messengers from the Shades to destroy the true love of a living couple—the messengers themselves had been selfish lovers while on earth. When things go wrong, the Devil himself intervenes, but is eventually defeated. The character of Berry's Devil—truculent, overbearing, dictatorial—was reputedly based on the scenarist Jacques Prévert's conception of Hitler and the film was originally planned to be set in modern times, but was eventually put back to the Fifteenth century to avoid making the allegorical parallels too obvious in the then dangerous circumstances. Satan appears in a minor capacity in *The Undead* (1957, *dir.* Roger Corman), a rather tedious affair about an experimen-

Horrifying and hilarious: WITCHCRAFT
THROUGH THE AGES

talist in time who picks up a prostitute, transports her back a thousand years, has afterwards to return himself to save her from execution, and then finds himself implanted in the Middle Ages: he is also present by implication, of course, in the various films dealing with "possession," and in those on witchcraft mentioned below.

The "old religion" has been the subject of numerous horror films, mostly superficial in their treatment of the subject. A number of more serious studies may be considered here. As

168

early as 1909 Edison made *In the Days of Witchcraft*, in which a Puritan girl is burnt at the stake, but the first and still most detailed inquiry into the practices is Benjamin Christensen's *Witchcraft through the Ages* (1922), which is a sort of compendium of every aspect of the craft. The director himself is a fine rumbustious Devil, and the film, with its wild orgies, lewd old women, spells, cavortings, potions, and black magical rites, is by turns horrifying and hilarious—as gripping today as when it first appeared. A modern episode bringing psychoanalysis to bear on "possession" is much weaker than the rest, but too brief to spoil the whole. The film has recently been re-released with a soundtrack.

Edgar G. Ulmer's *The Black Cat* is vaguely concerned with witchcraft, and introduces Satanic rites, but these are interrupted before they have made much progress, and the participants, in full evening dress, are clearly not going to let themselves go very far. *Maid of Salem* (1927, *dir.* Frank Lloyd) is based on the famous New England Trials of 1692. Its approach is interesting in that the strong atmosphere of evil menace which is conjured up stems not from the so-called witches and their superstitious practices but from the fear and bigoted cruelty of their hunters. As the unpleasant little girl who pretends to be possessed and by her accusations starts the reign of terror, Bonita Granville is frighteningly convincing. Devil-worship in New York's Greenwich Village is the subject of *The Seventh Victim* (1943, *dir.* Mark Robson) in which the producer Val Lewton's flair for suggesting horror underlying the everyday is well in evidence.

The same year saw a much more important film, Carl Dreyer's beautiful and terrifying *Day of Wrath,* based on the well-known play by Wiers Jensen, *Anne Pedersdotter,* from which John Masefield also derived his work *The Witch.* Dreyer is not mainly concerned with the problem of witchcraft, which he uses to intensify the story of an illicit love between Anne, the young wife of the respected pastor, Hr. Absolon, and his son by a former marriage, Martin. Nevertheless, the shadow of the cult overshadows all the action. Martin has been away from home for years, and returns on the exact day on which an old woman has been accused of witchcraft and has appealed to the girl as one who is herself the daughter of a witch. The appeal fails. Foretelling the girl's own disaster, the old woman is burned—in a scene which horrifyingly combines the sweet singing of choir-boys and the smoke and crackle of the pyre. Martin and Anne are watching the scene, and terror and dread drive her into his arms at the exact moment of the woman's death. Later, Anne tells Absolon that she has never loved him, and when he dies from a heart attack she is herself accused of witchcraft by Absolon's mother who has always resented her. Such is the all-pervading dread of the cult and belief in its power, that the young man himself begins to suspect her—and finally Anne believes it might indeed be true. The whole pace of the film is relentlessly slow, and the grim drama of dark superstition and delusion is worked out in settings and costumes of austere beauty, and interiors resembling an exquisite series of old paintings—even though the photography is in black-and-white. As in *The Passion of Joan of Arc*, Dreyer makes much use of large close-ups, dwelling on such contrasts as that between the seamed, kindly yet ruthless face of Absolon and the softly rounded features of his girl-wife—the plump, smooth, suspicious face of Absolon's respectable mother and the flushed, anxiously quivering yet far from "sweet-old-womanly" appearance of the witch.

In *Black Magic* (1947, *dir.* Gregory Ratoff), Orson Welles appears as Cagliostro. The film, a grandiose Italian spectacle, travesties history, but is quite entertaining with its magical melodramatics and general skulduggery. *The Sorceress* (1955,

THE WITCHES OF SALEM (Simone Signoret at right)

dir. André Michel) concerns a supposed witch in a Scandinavian village who foresees her own death, falls unwisely in love, and is maltreated by the locals. The film's main interest is its indication of the ease with which quite genuine religious fervour can be perverted into bigoted intolerance, and thence to actual physical cruelty.

The Witches of Salem (*Les Sorcières de Salem*, 1957, *dir.* Raymond Rouleau) returns to the Massachusetts trials for its subject, though this was used by Arthur Miller (from whose play *The Crucible* the film is adapted) to point a comparison with the contemporary McCarthyism in America. As further adapted by Sartre, it is given an even wider significance, but

171

like butter on bread, the more it is spread the thinner it becomes. It is a film which has disappointed the high expectations aroused before its appearance. As a study in witchcraft or demoniac possession it is unconvincing and, though much violence is introduced, the scenes which should really shock are oddly weak, particularly the "Sabbath" which fails to arouse even the mildest *frisson*.

Witch-burning forms an important episode in *The Seventh Seal* (see Chapter Eight). The accused is a girl of fourteen, with cropped hair and "a pale, childish face." As she is carried in a cart to her place of execution, the Knight asks if it is true that she has been in league with the Devil. She nods quietly, and when the Knight replies that he too wants to meet the Devil, to ask him about God, she bids him look into her eyes.

The young "witch" of THE SEVENTH SEAL

But the Knight sees only emptiness, a dumb fear. The girl says she is not afraid of the fire, the Devil will protect her from all evil. The Knight gives her a draught to ease her pain. His Squire, Jöns, demands: "Who watches over that child? Is it the angels, or God, or the Devil, or only emptiness? Emptiness, my Lord." When the Knight protests, the Squire replies: "Look at her eyes. Her poor brain has just made a discovery. Emptiness under the moon." As the two depart, the eyes of the young "witch" close. There is no answer given. It is one of the most moving sequences in this great film.

Sensationalism returns with *Black Sunday* (1960) the first film to be directed by the Italian Mario Bava, who has since become noted for his baroque horrors. Derived from a folk story by the Russian writer Gogol, it concerns the tradition that one day in every hundred years Satan is allowed to roam the world in freedom—the day witches return to life in order to revenge themselves for their execution. Although essentially a horror film, it is said to be distinguished by imaginative treatment and to treat its superstitious subject seriously, but it has only just been permitted a public showing in England. Also banned are nearly all the witchcraft sequences of Roger Corman's *Masque of the Red Death* (1964), but the gathering of the messengers of Death is most impressively handled. Two other films of similar *genre* which nevertheless have some regard for the traditions and conventions of the subject are *Witchcraft* (1964, *dir.* Don Sharp) and *The Witches* (1966, *dir.* Cyril Frankel). The latter in particular, from the Hammer studios, presents an almost credible picture of black magic and diabolical conjuration in an English village—complete with a would-be clergyman (failed) who wears clerical garb and has a room set up as his personal chapel, including recorded organ music. This theme of a yearning for a religious calling thwarted and turned sour lends depth to a fairly commonplace story of

173

pins-in-dolls, suddenly menacing flocks of sheep, unaccountable maladies, withdrawn children and odd recluses.

A little-known film of considerable merit and seriousness on the theme of demoniac possession is Brunello Rondi's *Il Demonio* (1963). It is set in rural Southern Italy and concerns a girl, powerfully played by Daliah Lavi, who is haunted by diabolical voices and horrifying nightmares. She falls violently in love with a farmer and when, frightened off by her intensity, he marries another girl, she tries to put spells on them both. When found out, she is attacked by the villagers, runs away, and is raped by a shepherd. Finally the farmer gives way to her importunities, but in the morning kills her. The most striking scene is that in which the local priest tries to exorcise the demon, and the girl attacks him violently, speaking in an unknown tongue—there is real terror here, and although throughout the film the sexual basis of much religious and anti-religious "possession" is uncompromisingly demonstrated this aspect is never treated for its sensational value. Nor can everything be explained away, as it implies quite clearly, by the jargon of psycho-analysis.

One or two light-hearted essays in Witchcraft are mentioned in the following chapter, and no account would be complete without reference to the "Night on the Bare Mountain" section of Walt Disney's *Fantasia*. Set to Rimsky-Korsakov's orchestration of Moussorgsky's original tone poem, this animated depiction of a witches' Sabbath is one of the best episodes in the generally uneven and overrated medley.

Apart from the occasional use of seances to heighten the tension of thrillers, spiritualism seems to have inspired few films, and those are generally concerned with the exposure of trickery. As early as 1913 a film was made by Douglas Payne

Left, demoniac possession: Daliah Lavi in IL DEMONIO

entitled *Fraudulent Spiritualism Exposed,* and the only merit of a thriller of 1948 *The Spiritualist* (*dir.* Bernard Vorhaus) is the interesting detail into which it goes in exposing fraudulent practitioners. The one really notable film on the subject is Carlo-Menotti's own version of his opera *The Medium* (1951). This is an almost wholly successful example of the difficult combination of opera and film—after the first few moments the artificiality becomes altogether acceptable—as it did indeed with the very different *Umbrellas of Cherbourg,* over which *The Medium* has the advantage that the voices are those of the actual players. It is a terrifying warning against the dishonest exploitation of the pathetic faith of the bereaved and the lonely, and even had the film as a whole been much less satisfactory it would have justified itself in perpetuating the tremendous performance of Marie Powers. As the fake medium who feels a hand touch her throat in the middle of a seance, and is torn by doubt as to whether this was a supernatural manifestation or a human trick, her presence towers over the screen. The key moment of the film, perhaps, occurs when, having shouted at her three regular clients that they never saw their dead loved ones, that it is all fake, that they have been fooled, and that they must get out and never come back, she is faced by their unbreakable certainty, their bland refusal to admit what they have been actually *shown* to be false, their genuine surprise at her terror. "But why be afraid—afraid of our dead?" they ask as she drives them out. To that question, she indeed knows the answer. To the other—was it a trick?—she tries frantically to obtain a reply. Mentally and physically, she crumbles. In a moment of drunken terror, she shoots the mute gypsy boy who has helped her run the seances (and whom she suspects),

Right, a child's father figure:
JULIET OF THE SPIRITS

176

mistaking him for a ghost. As she crouches over his body, uselessly beseeching, "Was it you?" the film closes.

The nightmare effect that certain aspects of religious teaching can have on children is an important theme in Fellini's *Juliet of the Spirits* (1965). Memories of a gruesome and, one would have thought, totally unsuitable convent school play in which an eight-year-old girl takes part, haunt her long after she is a grown woman in distorted and terrifying forms. Representing a martyr who is grilled alive, the little girl is raised on a pulley high to the ceiling of the stage, presumably representing her soul's ascent to Heaven, while the other children chant a doleful dirge. In memory God becomes a dark, sinister, elongated figure behind a blank door in the domed roof, the convent nuns a row of black, faceless, cowled figures moving in a menacing, relentless procession, her own child-self a grotesque, obscene parody of innocence.

Children also feature largely in two of Jack Clayton's films, *The Innocents* (1961) and *Our Mother's House* (1967). The former, from the play based on Henry James's famous ghost story *The Turn of the Screw*, concerns the possession of two young children by the evil spirits of two servants after their death. The apparently unavoidable question as to whether it is all in the mind of the governess in charge of them is really academic. As the film is made, we *see* the possession and, under Clayton's brilliant handling, a very terrifying experience it is. *Our Mother's House* shows the effect a narrow and over-strict religious upbringing may have on a family of children. Throughout their mother's long illness the seven children—all young—have lived with her in a rambling, decaying suburban house, alone except for a sluttish daily woman. Knowing little of reality in their self-contained world, and thinking, when she dies, that they will be placed in an orphanage, they bury her body in the garden and set up a sort of chapel to her spirit in

178

a shed which they furnish with her personal relics and furniture from her bedroom. There they gather at night by the light of candles. The eldest girl, Diana, rocks herself into a "trance" and communicates with her mother to learn her will. Encouraged by the faith of the others, she works herself into a state of complete possession—and possessiveness. Eventually, unconsciously jealous of a smaller girl, who is proud of her long hair and has been using her mother's comb on it, Diana ruthlessly commands (on orders she has "received") that the hair must be cut off. In a truly unnerving scene this is done. The little girl's resultant nervous illness prompts inquiries from the outside world, in the person of their schoolmistress. They are temporarily saved by the completely unexpected arrival of the father, and their enclosed existence opens out. Clayton succeeds in making credible what might have seemed an improbable situation throughout—in particular the formidable scenes of the children coldly quoting Biblical texts at one another, ruthlessly putting into practice the teaching they have received as interpreted by their literal minds. The closing moments are poignant, and the director shows his sensitivity in creating this strange, haunting film without resorting to the easy sentimentality of conventional childish charm.

10. The Lighter Side: Comedy and Fantasy

FILMS IN WHICH THE COMEDY is in the situation rather than the whimsicalities of the clerical character are comparatively rare. Most famous of all is Charlie Chaplin's *The Pilgrim* (1923), in which Chaplin as an escaping convict grabs a minister's clothes while the latter is bathing, is welcomed by waiting Elders at the station and has to sustain the part. It is odd now to recall the shocked indignation with which the film was originally received in some quarters. A funny parson—enacting a funny sermon—taking up a funny collection: "vulgar, distasteful, offensive" were words used to describe the situation. *Tempora mutantur . . .* In fact it is among the best early Chaplins and contains, in the mimed sermon of David and Goliath, one of his most brilliant inspirations. Harry Langdon in *The Strong Man* and Harold Lloyd in *For Heaven's Sake* (both 1926) each come to the rescue of troubled Missions, as does Chaplin himself, less directly, in *Easy Street* (1917).

A charming little comedy built round an important occasion of a little girl's life is the Italian film *First Communion* directed in 1950 by Alessandro Blasetti, with Aldo Fabrizi, priest of *Open City,* as the girl's proud father. The entire action passes in under two hours of an Easter morning. Though a lightweight trifle concerning the non-delivery of the girl's white dress, it is sharpened by occasional touches of satire at the absurdities and pomposities of human behaviour, and the total effect is wholly delightful.

In the main, however, situation comedy is confined to isolated episodes in otherwise secular films. "Funny wedding

Left: Charlie Chaplin as THE PILGRIM

scenes" are of course innumerable (there are even one or two
"funny funerals"), and most people will have their own special
memories: from silent days, perhaps, Raymond Griffith as the
groom in *The Night Club* (1925, *dir.* Paul Tribe, Frank Ur-
son), glancing nervously round during the ceremony to see if
his eligibility will be challenged a second time; Reginald Denny
as the unwilling fake clergyman in *What Happened to Jones*
(1925, *dir.* William A. Seiter), desperately hoping someone *will*
interrupt the service he does not want to perform ("Doesn't
anyone here present know of any just cause . . . ?") There is
also the unforgettable *Seven Chances* of Buster Keaton, with
determined brides arriving at the church in their thousands to
secure both husband and fortune. More recently the ancient
gags of nervous couple, embarrassed or emotional families,
wedding-ring fumblings and general solemn tension were re-
vivified with beautiful timing in Roy Boulting's *The Family
Way* (1966). There is the wedding of Richard Petruchio Burton and Elizabeth Katherina Taylor, outrageously and up-
roariously interpolated into *The Taming of the Shrew* (1967,
dir. Franco Zeffirelli), a brilliant few minutes of perfectly
judged broad comedy, crowned by Giancarlo Cobelli's brief,
unforgettable appearance as the bewildered and finally frantically wedlocking priest.

In the hilarious finale of *The Graduate* (1967, *dir.* Mike
Nichols) the young man (Dustin Hoffman) rescues his beloved
from a wedding worse than death by wielding the power of
the Cross, quite literally, to foil his enemies: a scene which
avoids offence by the sheer sympathy which has been en-
gendered for the nice, desperate hero, and the totally un-
Christian viciousness of his opponents. In the circumstances his
action appears both justifiable and exhilarating.

The one memorable "funny funeral" is undoubtedly that
in René Clair's *avant-garde* cine-poem *Entr'acte* (1924), in

182

which the procession starts slowly with becoming gravity, the pace gradually quickens, the hearse slips away down a slope, the mourners start to run, then to sprint, until with a wealth of parallel images the whole affair mounts to a climax of speed and confusion. The same idea of the danger of a crack in the solemn *facade* is used in *What a Way To Go,* where a momentary loss of footing by one of the pallbearers brings the entire *cortège,* after a gallant attempt at recovery, hurtling down a curving flight of stairs—a brief pre-title sequence which is one of the most amusing in the film. Not to be overlooked, too, is the satirical cremation giving the protagonist a new lease of life in *Decline and Fall . . . of a Bird-watcher* (1968, *dir.* John Krish).

It is in the realm of fantasy, however, that most "religious" comedies have their origins. One of the better examples is Vincente Minnelli's *Cabin in the Sky* (1941), an all-Negro fantasy which is a sort of musical *Green Pastures,* though lacking the imagination and dignity of that fine film. The story concerns a man who is badly hurt in a drunken fight and, while lying between life and death, sees the powers of good and evil battling for his soul. The music, by Duke Ellington and others, helps to offset some rather soggy slabs of whimsy.

Death appears in the form of Fredric March in *Death Takes a Holiday* (1934, *dir.* Mitchell Leisen), as a man of the world who falls in love and, after his "holiday" during which no-one and nothing dies, returns whence he came accompanied by the girl because she has come to love rather than to fear him. In *On Borrowed Time* (1939, *dir.* Harold S. Bucquet) he is impersonated by Cedric Hardwicke and imprisoned in the branches of a magic tree, from which he can only descend if asked to do so.

The Devil, in his various forms, turns up in a number of fantastic or allegorical comedies. As Lucifer in Ernst Lubitsch's

183

Heaven Can Wait (1943), he listens to a man's story of his life before considering where he should be accommodated after it. Though minor Lubitsch, and made after his great days, it contains quite a lot of the director's old elegance and sparkle. *In Meet Mr. Lucifer* (1953, *dir.* Anthony Pelissier), Stanley Holloway doubles the role of the Devil with that of an actor, Mr. Hollingsworth, who while playing the Demon King in pantomime falls through a trap door and finds himself in the nether regions. The film is a light-hearted attack on television—a diabolical invention by which Lucifer hopes to spread misery and disunity around the world. Claude Rains in *Here Comes Mr. Jordan* (1941, *dir.* Alexander Hall) is a supernatural Being in charge of a Heavenly airport from which people set off on their final journey to the Elysian Fields. He also has the power to arrange for the transmigration of souls into other bodies. A boxer killed in an accident proves his case that death was premature, and is allowed to return in various forms. A dubious subject, dubiously treated.

The Devil's Eye (1960) is an Ingmar Bergman comedy. The Devil has a stye in his eye, caused by the sight of a chaste woman. He therefore sends Don Juan down—or up—to deprive her of her virginity. The Don, however, as might be foreseen, falls in love with the girl and leaves her inviolate. The girl marries her *fiancé*, but on her wedding night tells him she has never even kissed another man. This lie (for Don Juan had at least got that far) and the fact of her consummating her marriage, are sufficient to cure the Devil's eye. A sub-plot concerns the girl's mother—the frustrated wife of a pastor—who is seduced by the Don's servant. There is also an old Devil who accompanies Don Juan as a sort of watch-dog, and is shut up in a cupboard by the pastor; and a highly original being called an Ear Devil, who eavesdrops on the girl's wedding night and torments the Don by recounting what he hears. A

*THE DEVIL'S EYE: the Devil and Don Juan
(Stig Järrel and Jarl Kulle)*

not very convincing Hell is situated in a tastefully furnished drawing-room with flames leaping around outside the windows. Stig Järrel, the unforgettable sadistic schoolmaster of *Frenzy*, is a quite impressive Devil. The film is divided into three clear "acts," each introduced by a Narrator—thus deliberately alienating the spectator from any great involvement—and is described as a Rondo Capriccioso. It is lightweight Bergman but, as could be expected, seriousness keeps breaking in, particularly in the relationship between the pastor and his wife, the aridity of whose marriage is treated with sympathy and compassion.

Comedy angels, of both sexes, abound—though for some reason do not seem to have made much headway until the coming of sound. In *I Married an Angel* (1942, *dir*. W. S. van Dyke) Jeanette MacDonald appears as a musical "angel," singing lustily, if not particularly divinely, at Nelson Eddy. Described as "demure, coquettish, glamorous and saintly" she proves enough, if not too much, of a good thing. Charles Kemper is the angelic figure in *An Angel Comes to Brooklyn* (1946). Formerly a conjuror, he helps to find theatrical engagements for his friends still on earth. What the worldly ten-per-centers have to say about this is not recorded, but the whole affair is rather enjoyably silly, and no doubt would have a considerable appeal to all members of Equity. An angelic Western, *Heaven Only Knows* (1947, *dir.* Albert S. Rogell) in which the Archangel Michael is sent down to put matters right for a man who has been allowed to exist without a soul and miss his appointed destiny, is distinguished by the unusual critical unanimity in deploring its lack of taste. Three more heavenly visitants during this very angelic period were Leon Ames in *Yolanda and the Thief* (1946, *dir.* Vincente Minnelli), Henry Travers in *It's a Wonderful Life* (1947, *dir.* Frank Capra), and Cary Grant in *The Bishop's Wife* (1948, *dir.* Henry Koster). The first of this trio shows Fred Astaire as a debonair con man persuading the richest girl in a mythical country that he is her guardian angel (in reality Leon Ames) with whom she has been communicating on the telephone. It is embarrassingly whimsical and quite lacking in the usual Minnelli flair. Much more satisfying is the Capra film, a bitter-sweet comedy with many vintage moments. George Bailey (James Stewart), ruined and sick of life, is wishing he had never been born and contemplating suicide. Clarence, an angel, is dispatched to deter him and to show what would have happened to his family and friends if in fact his selfish wish had been granted. Meanwhile everyone bands together to help him out of his difficulties in more material matters. The usual Capra comments on human and spiritual values are as pointed and valid as ever, and a highly entertaining story combines the natural and the super-

186

natural with rare success. *The Bishop's Wife* is another moral fantasy handled with unusual charm, in which an angel—delightfully named Dudley—comes to the aid of a bishop who is so taken up with his plans for building a Cathedral that he has lost the common touch with his flock.

Jack Benny in *The Horn Blows at Midnight* (1948, *dir.* Raoul Walsh) dreams that he is an angel trumpeter (presumably Gabriel) who is to destroy the earth by sounding his instrument at midnight. The film is an uncomfortable mixture of pop and piety. On about the same level is *For Heaven's Sake* (1950, *dir.* George Seaton), not to be confused with Harold Lloyd's comedy of the same title. Two angels, Edmund Gwenn and, of all people, Clifton Webb, arrive on earth to repair a theatrical producer's broken marriage. The partnership, however, is saved by less celestial means when the wife discovers she is going to have a baby. The film is probably unique in that one of the angels appears in the guise of a Texas ranger.

In contrast, *The Angel Who Pawned Her Harp* (1954, *dir.* Alan Bromly) is a rather charming little English tale of an angle in Islington—the Angel district, of course—who finds that she is short of money and pawns her harp. This naturally involves her in the troubles and problems of the pawnbroker and his associates, and leads to a course of generally doing good all round. The whimsy is a little overpowering at times, the treatment a little weighty for so light a piece—even so there are some pleasant, even touching moments, notably in the scenes between the Angel and the solitary old broker as played by Diane Cilento and Felix Aylmer.

A miraculous fantasy, described as a fable for grown-up children, is Vittorio De Sica's *Miracle in Milan* (1951). The story concerns the spirit of a kind old lady who befriends a group of vagabonds eking out a bare existence in a crude village by a railway embankment near Milan. When oil is discovered on the site, the millionaire owner wants to drive them off, but the old lady gives a white dove to a foundling she had brought up when on earth. The dove—the equivalent of the fairy wand—enables the foundling, Totò, to have anything he wants, and to repulse the invaders. But the dove is removed, and Totò and the beggars are imprisoned. However, the old lady returns the magic bird to him, he obtains a number of brooms, and all the beggars ride off on them into the sky, to a better land where "good day really means good day." This grim underlying theme, that only the rich and greedy can survive, and the meek, far from inheriting the earth, can only hope to ride away to a never-never land, is softened by De Sica to a gentle fairy story, but its submerged presence gives a cutting edge to the film that removes it from the realm of "mere" fantasy.

The lighter side of witchcraft is seen at its best in René Clair's *I Married a Witch*, wherein the soul of a sorceress, reincarnated in the fascinating Veronica Lake, causes her to fall in love with Fredric March and wreak havoc in both his private and public life. With Cecil Kellaway in attendance as a warlock, this is one of Clair's wittiest and most lasting Hollywood comedies. Less entertaining is Richard Quine's *Bell, Book and Candle* (1958), adapted from John van Druten's play, though the use of modern inventions such as the telephone by present-day witches in the practice of their black art is amusing. Two childhood witches demand mention, Disney's in *Snow White and the Seven Dwarfs* (1937) and Margaret Hamilton's in *The Wizard of Oz* (1940, *dir.* Victor Fleming). The latter is a genuinely demoniac creation, splendidly sinister throughout and particularly in her moment of dissolution.

Finally there is the only notable spiritualist comedy, David Lean's production of *Blithe Spirit* (1945) adapted from Noël Coward's play, in which Margaret Rutherford—looking oddly like a bewigged Michel Simon—splendidly hearty and eccentric as the enthusiastic medium who causes chaos in the life of the writer Charles Condomine by conjuring up the ghosts of his first, and later his second, deceased wives. The original play, and presumably the film, was received with reserve in some spiritualistic circles at first, but it is difficult to believe that so mild a joke could give lasting offence. The film is little more than recorded theatre, old-fashioned even in the year of its appearance.

The above is, of course, only a selection of the more relevant fantastic and supernatural films. Ghosts, walking undead, zombies and other perturbed spirits stalk the ground in large numbers just beyond the fairly wide net we have cast.

11. Satirical Comment

WHENEVER THE "ANTI-RELIGIOUS" FILM is mentioned the name of Luis Buñuel inevitably, relentlessly, crops up. So much prominence, indeed, is given to this aspect of his work that much else—his wit, humour, deep humanity, sense of beauty (there have been few visually lovelier films than *Belle de Jour*)—is apt to be overlooked. It has been asserted that a man who spends so much time attacking the tenets of religion must "believe in them"—as fruitless an argument as that about the atheist who exclaims "Good God!" Buñuel speaks through his films. In *Un Chien Andalou,* made with Salvador Dali in 1928, two priests are dragged along the floor by a young man together with other lumber, symbols of the dead weight of early clerical teaching which he is compelled to lug around inside his personality. In *L'Age d'Or* (1930) a party of Bishops is seen invading a rocky coast and celebrating Mass—later they are a bundle of dried-up skeletons, still clad in mitre and robe, still humbly saluted by passing dignitaries. Towards the close of the film the Duc de Blangis, one of the dissolute "heroes" of De Sade, emerges from an artificial castle (an obvious film set) strongly resembling the conventional portraits of Christ. In *El* (1952) the insane man's jealous delusions cause him to imagine while in church during Mass that the celebrant, acolytes and congregation are laughing and jeering at him. Violent cutting from his wild imaginings to sober reality and back end by imparting a wholly ridiculous air to the ceremonial. In *Robinson Crusoe* (1952), the hero in his agonising loneliness cries out to the mountains "My soul! My soul . . . " and is answered only by empty echoes. In *La Mort en ce Jardin* (1956), the priest who tries to follow Christ's teaching brings down disaster on himself and others. When for a short time, under stress of

NAZARIN: the disillusionment of a priest

danger, he acts more like a man than a priest—e.g. in such symbolic acts as ripping up a prayer-book to keep going a fire which is succouring a party of refugees—he becomes of some use to his fellow beings; when he reverts, he becomes once again helpless, and ironically meets his death at the hands of a religious fanatic he himself has helped to create.

This theme of the impracticability, or even culpable uselessness of Christian conduct in real life is the most frequent in films which are critical of religious thought or practice. Both *Nazarin* (1958) and *Viridiana* (1961), two of Buñuel's best-known films, enlarge on it. In the former a Mexican Catholic priest decides it is his duty to follow Christian precepts literally. The period is about sixty years ago. In a whole series of incidents, starting from his offer of shelter to a

191

prostitute wanted by the police, he discovers that absolute adherence to the teaching of Jesus leads to trouble, unhappiness, and his own utter disillusionment. Eventually he is arrested as the accomplice of the prostitute in her crime of murder. He is maltreated and imprisoned in a chain gang. On the road an old woman offers him a pineapple. Reduced to the utmost misery, he humbly accepts. This final gesture has been interpreted by some as indicative of Nazarin's recovery of his beliefs through a small act of charity, and therefore of a change of attitude in Buñuel himself, but the opposite explanation is at least as valid—that Nazarin at last gratefully acknowledges the values of the material world. Between *Nazarin* and *Viridiana* Buñuel made *The Young One*, ridiculously and misleadingly re-titled *Island of Shame*. This is a small-scale work of charm and subtlety. It is concerned with the conflicts of innocence and prejudice (including racial prejudice) rather than with religion, but even here the one thoroughly unsympathetic character, far less likable than the racist game-warden, is the pastor—thin-lipped, moralising, prissy, cold, who while mouthing platitudes against discrimination orders his mattress to be turned because a coloured man has previously rested on it.

In *Viridiana* the theme of *Nazarin* is revived in a much more complex film. A young girl about to take her vows reluctantly agrees to pay a last visit to her uncle. Overcome by the likeness between the girl and his wife who died on their wedding night, he persuades Viridiana to put on the dead woman's bridal dress, and has her drugged preparatory to seducing her. When the moment comes he shrinks from the deed, and the next morning hangs himself. Viridiana, suffering feelings

*Right, the Last Supper:
top, KING OF KINGS (1927);
below, the parody—VIRIDIANA*

192

of guilt at his death, takes over the dead man's estate and tries to run it on Christian principles. Once again, disaster and horror result. The climax of the film is an obscene orgy staged by a band of filthy beggars whom she has befriended. During the absence of herself and the illegitimate son of her uncle with whom she runs the place, the beggars run riot. Viridiana returns to a scene of nightmare filth and terror. The house is a shambles, and, with a gramophone blaring out anthems from Handel's *Messiah*, one of the most loathsome of the tramps assaults her. The ending, bereft of even the small gesture of decency to be found in *Nazarin,* shows Viridiana, her spirituality totally destroyed, joining in a game of cards with her cousin and his present mistress. The famous parody of Da Vinci's *Last Supper* occurs during the orgy, "photographed" by an old woman obscenely raising her skirts at the posed group, but throughout the film the attack is pressed home. Yet the final effect is not one of negation, rather the opposite. Compassion uninformed by clarity of thought can lead only to disaster. Christianity is not enough.

Buñuel has said of *The Exterminating Angel* (1962) that it cannot be rationally explained, and it certainly provides a field-day for interpreters and symbol-hunters. The basic plot, if such it can be called, is simple. A wealthy gentleman and his wife have invited a party of guests to supper after a visit to the opera. For some reason, the servants in the house are nervous and ill-at-ease. Oddness sets in early, as we are shown the arrival of the guests twice, and with slight differences. By the time the meal is finished all the servants have left, except one, the major-domo. The guests themselves seem strangely reluctant to leave, and spend the night in their host's salon. Next morning neither they nor the major-domo, José, are *able* to go, though the wall that prevents them, apparently stretching down the centre of the chamber, is non-existent. They remain in their invisible imprisonment for weeks, until they are reduced to filth, hunger, fighting and utter degradation. Every *façade* of civilised living is broken down, and their situation remains inexplicable. Their escape from it is equally inexplicable when one of their number suddenly realises they are in exactly the same positions as when their restriction began. She takes them back over what they said and did, and they find themselves free. A few days later they are in church giving thanks for their release, only to find that this time not only they themselves, but the priest and the rest of the congregation are similarly trapped, in the church. The film can be regarded as a stripping away of veneers from upper-class polite society—and it is noticeable that the one remaining servant is in the upper strata of the servant hierarchy. He has also, it is pointed out, been brought up by Jesuits. The sheep that wander into the salon and are butchered to save the inmates from starvation have obvious connotations. The second, and apparently final, immurement occurs in a church itself. The "angel" itself may be, as Raymond Durgnat says, "the spiritual climate of bourgeois conformism, drawn to its (desired) conclusion of inner paralysis," but it is constricting to confine anything in the film to any specific significance.

Simon of the Desert (1965) is a short modern study of the famous Stylite, or pillar-hermit. The period is indeterminate. He is seen in his connections with the local people, during which such typically Buñuel incidents occur as that of the thief whose severed hands are miraculously restored by the Saint, and who at once uses them once again in the same criminal activities. The main thread of events concerns the temptation of the Saint by the Devil in a number of unusual guises—all of them played by the actress Silvia Pinal. The first is a precocious pig-tailed school girl, the second an effete

Temptation: SIMON OF THE DESERT

hermaphrodite, a bewhiskered soprano-voiced "Good Shep-herd," the third a beatnik girl who arrives in a self-propelled coffin. He is taken off his pillar in an aeroplane by this last girl, and lands up in a low jive-dive where he is told he is to spend the rest of his time sitting watching the dancers. The modern witches' Sabbath is, in fact, a sort of permanent beat session. The film is full of the usual entertaining am-biguities and is notable for its entrancing black-and-white photography (by Gabriel Figueroa), in particular one unfor-gettable long-held shot of the solitary figure on his isolated

196

pillar in the distance with sandstorm clouds wreathing across the screen in grey patterns around him.

Buñuel's latest film, *Belle de Jour* (1967) concerns a young housewife who, to satisfy her masochistic inclinations, starts to work in a brothel during the afternoons when her husband is absent. It contains one moment of clear blasphemous intent. As the young wife nervously climbs the stairs to the brothel she has a memory, briefly shown in a flashback, of herself as a child shrinking away from the proffered Host at her first communion: as Dilys Powell describes it, "another sacrifice of the body." The film is a visually exquisite example of Buñuel's unique commingling of the fantastic and the real, with an ending which is equivocal and yet is wholly satisfying and fulfilled.

Federico Fellini's attitude to the Church has an ambivalence which is interestingly discussed by Suzanne Budgen who devotes a whole chapter to the subject in her book on the director. In addition to *Juliet of the Spirits* (see page 178), we may note the notorious Christ-carrying helicopter opening of *La Dolce Vita* (1960)—and the film's mysterious close; the convincingly priest-masquerading crooks in *Il Bidone* (1955); the incongruous monks in *I Vitelloni* (1953); and the Saraghina episode in *8½* (1963) which, in Suzanne Budgen's words "suggests a rigidity in the church which completely fails to take account of the love and grace which operate outside it."

Several French directors have tilted their lance at the religious windmill. Jean Vigo's anarchistic *Zéro de Conduite* (1933), an outburst against the oppression of petty tyranny symbolised in a boys' school, contains a parody of a religious procession in which, after a riot in their dormitory, the boys move down the long room in night dresses like church vestments, showered with an incense of feathers from burst pillows, while their snooping duty-master, strapped to his bed, is raised on high and angled after the manner of a holy statue. The sequence, shot in slow motion, has an unearthly, hypnotic beauty which heightens the processional effect. *Zéro de Conduite* was banned from public showing for over ten years.

The Virtuous Isidore, from a story by Guy de Maupassant, has a Buñuel-like theme—that "goodness" is intolerable. A guileless young villager is given the annual prize for virtue by local dignitaries because no girl is found sufficiently chaste to receive it. Weighed down by the burden of his reputation, he breaks out, spends the prize money on a wild drunken spree and ends up wholly disgraced in the eyes of the righteously horrified elders. Fernandel in the 1932 version lent the character a gentle dignity which gave depth and humanity to the lighthearted comedy, but Jean Boyer's 1950 re-make with Bourvil sacrificed sensitivity to broad slapstick. The same story, *Le Rosier de Mme. Husson,* served as the basis for Benjamin Britten's opera *Albert Herring.*

Fernandel also appears in Claude Autant-Lara's *The Red Inn* (1951), playing the part of a monk who is among a party of travellers taking shelter in the Inn of the title. While there, he learns that the owners are in the habit of murdering customers for their wealth. The monk is powerless to do anything to help his fellow-travellers. At last, a monkey belonging to a former visitor escapes and, arousing the suspicions of the police, causes the arrest of the innkeeper. Happily, the monk speeds the monkey-saved coachload on their way. A Negro servant of the innkeeper's, however, saws away a support of a bridge, and the coach and passengers crash to their destruction. The monk goes mad. The film, conceived in terms of black farce, is a fierce satire on the Church, dwelling once again on the helplessness of its followers when up against the practical problems of this world.

Georges Franju brought upon himself the disapproval of the

Catholic Central Office ("that miserable organisation") for his film of François Mauriac's *Thérèse Desqueyroux* (1962), and had more trouble with them over the scene in *Judex* (1963) where the villainess (Francine Bergé) strips off the nun's habit she has been wearing as a disguise. Raymond Durgnat, who examines this aspect of Franju's approach in parts of his study of the director (Studio Vista, 1968), also sees an inverted theology in *Eyes without a Face* (1959), though it is doubtful whether any analogies would strike the average viewer of this horrific and beautiful film. The equivocal *Notre Dame, Cathédrale de Paris* is referred to in Chapter Six.

In *God Is My Co-Pilot* 1945, (*dir.* Robert Florey), a Catholic priest is shown reassuring a conscience-stricked bomber-pilot that God is with him in the cockpit as he blasts his fellow beings to pieces. It is kindest to persuade oneself that this sickening film, with its gleeful gloating over the shooting down of enemy pilots and its nauseating alliance of religion and war, is satirically meant. Certainly it is a much more devastating criticism of the abuse of religion than many an obviously intentional attack.

Stanley Kramer's *Inherit the Wind* (1960), adapted from the play of the same title, is based on the famous Scopes Evolution Case, known popularly as the Dayton "monkey trial." A school teacher in the Fundamentalist territory of deep Tennessee is arrested for preaching evolution. Brady (in real life William Jennings Bryan) is nominated to prosecute, and Drummond (in real life Clarence Darrow) is retained by a newspaper to defend Cates (Scopes). In the film, as in real life, Cates is treated more or less as a puppet—a figure, unimportant in himself, on which a test case is to be built up. He is found guilty, as indeed he was bound to be, but Brady's Fundamentalist arguments have been so thoroughly discredited that a merely nominal fine is imposed. Still trying to justify his theories, Brady suddenly dies. The opposing standpoints are fairly and excitingly presented. Drummond obviously commands most sympathy, but Brady, despite his bigotry and narrowness, is depicted as a sincere and courageous, if not a likable man. Unfortunately, the film is fatally weakened towards the end by sentimental divergencies from the truth. Brady dies of a dramatic heart attack; Bryan, according to Clarence Darrow's biographer, "after eating one of his enormous dinners." Drummond (played by Spencer Tracy) is much affected by the death of a once-loved friend; Darrow's valedictory remark was, aloud, "His death is a great loss to the American people," and, *sotto voce*, "Broken heart nothing, he died of a busted belly." The film's worst betrayal, however, is Drummond's final gesture, when, after an absurd and unlikely speech contradicting everything he has so far supported, he picks up the Bible and a volume of Darwin from the courtroom table, places the two books comfortably together under his arm with a coy look, and walks slowly away. This trite piece of "symbolism" runs altogether contrary to the spirit of the film itself, and to the facts on which it is based—and is also the sort of dangerous over-simplification which is no help towards any reconciliation of divergent views.

The British *Heavens Above* (1963, *dir.* John Boulting) begins as yet another satire on putting Christian preaching into modern practice. Through a mistake in names, an uncompromising North country ex-prison chaplain is appointed to a tight little country parish in place of the easy-going socialite parson expected by the Lady of the Manor, and proceeds to create havoc by insisting on strict application of the principles in which he believes. Unfortunately the film lacks the courage of its own convictions, and degenerates into typical English rural farce, ending up with the parson taking the place of a nervous astronaut and singing hymns while orbiting around in a space rocket. *The Loved One* (1965, *dir.* Tony Richardson), based on the novel by Evelyn Waugh, selects as its target one aspect of religious extravagance, the American Way of Death. Like *Heavens Above*, it deserts satire for admittedly effective farce, ending with another rocket, this time conveying the first corpse to be given burial in celestial space. The very odd English production *Privilege* (1967, *dir.* Peter Watkins) concerns a pop singer who is taken up first by the government to channel the rebelliousness of young people into controllable grooves of hero-worshipping hysteria, and later by the Church to lead a "return to religion" through pop-type revivalism. Eventually he is betrayed by both. The film splashes vitriol around with indisputable sincerity—and indeed has some quite fiercely effective moments—but it never really comes to grips with the enemy, owing partly to over-gimmicky treatment, partly to the strait-jacket of its television-commentary approach, and partly to inadequate acting.

Finally, in *La Ricotta* (*Cream Cheese*, an episode in the portmanteau film *ROGOPAG*, 1963), Pier Paolo Pasolini exposes the insincerity and profane attitude of certain makers of Biblical films. (He himself, of course, is the director of *The Gospel According to St. Matthew*.) The scene represented in the making is the Crucifixion. The 'director' is Orson Welles. The actor playing the repentant thief ("Lord, remember me when Thou comest into Thy Kingdom"), is a middle-aged labourer, who is tormented and tantalised by the members of the cast and crew once they have secured him to his cross. The extra is ill, forced to work in order to provide for his family. The "jokes" of the rest become increasingly cruel and sadistic. They taunt him, withhold his food, Mary Magdalene does a striptease in front of him. The cream cheese of the title causes his death: deprived of his proper meal, he gulps the cheese down, and chokes on it. The unseen actor playing Christ, of course, lives on. As can be seen, the episode has political implications also. It resulted in the banning of the entire film, and Pasolini received a suspended prison sentence.

ROGOPAG has as its subject the attitude of commercial religious-film makers. Often this is held to be suspect, particularly in Hollywood, because their object is to make money. This argument, however, could be levelled at other forms of art with a religious theme, and provided money is not the *sole* object, it is not relevant. It hardly needs to be stated that many of the films discussed in this book, all of them made for a commercial market, are works of unquestioned sincerity and integrity; and even in others, box-office considerations have not been allowed entirely to swamp every other consideration. In particular regarding our perhaps somewhat jaundiced survey of the "religious spectacular," it is only fair to say that of all types of film this is one of the most difficult to bring off successfully in a commercial market. It must reimburse its generally enormous cost: so it must appeal to a mass audience. It has to feature one or more stars: so it has to be tailored to fit their personalities. It has to provide much superficially exciting action, so its stories must be elaborated or embellished. Throughout all the arts, myth, legend and story of early history have been similarly modified. Bearing in mind the additional difficulties and complexities with which the film has to contend, it is not remarkable that the still small voice is so seldom heard above the general din. The miracle is that, in spite of everything, such moments do occur; and this should be appreciated.

Appendix

NUMEROUS ORGANISATIONS and church groups also make or sponsor films of religious interest and content.

There are two religious film centres founded and maintained by the churches themselves:

International Protestant Film Centre
30, Borneolaan, Hilversum, Netherlands.
International Catholic Film Office
8 rue de l'Orme, Brussels 4, Belgium.

These centres have an information service about current films, and they also give annual awards to those films which "by their inspiration and quality contribute best to spiritual progress and development of human values."

In some countries, the National Christian Councils have sponsored films. Especially active are:

National Christian Council (Film Commission)
Interchurch Centre, 475 Riverside Drive,
New York, N.Y. 10027 U.S.A.
National Christian Council (Audio-Visual Commission)
4-13, Shibuya 4-Chrome, Shibuya-Ku, Tokyo, Japan.

Individual church groups in several countries also make films, and some have been recognised in International Film Festivals. Among these are the productions of:

Christian Aid, 10, Eaton Gate, London, S.W. 1, England.
Church of England (Church Missionary Society,
157, Waterloo Road, London, S.E.1.)
Lutheran Film Associates, 315 Park Avenue South,
New York, N.Y. 10027, U.S.A.
United Church of Canada (Berkeley Studio),
315 Queen St. E., Toronto 2, Ont. Canada
World Council of Churches (Information Department)
150, Route de Ferney, Geneva 20, Switzerland.

Select Bibliography

Bardèche, M., and Brassilach, R.: *History of the Film* (London, George Allen & Unwin, 1938)

Bergman, Ingmar: *A Film Trilogy* (London, Calder & Boyars, 1967)

Bergman, Ingmar: *Four Screenplays* (London, Secker & Warburg; New York, Simon & Schuster, 1960)

Budgen, Suzanne: *Fellini* (British Film Institute, 1966)

Connor, Edward: "Christ on the Screen," article in *Screen Facts*, number 16

Cowie, Peter: *Swedish Cinema* (London, A. Zwemmer; New York, A. S. Barnes & Co., 1966)

DeMille, Cecil B.: *Autobiography* (London, W. H. Allen, 1960)

Durgnat, Raymond: *Franju* (London, Studio Vista, 1967)

Durgnat, Raymond: *Luis Buñuel* (London, Studio Vista, 1967)

Estève, Michel (Ed.): *Jeanne d'Arc à l'Écran* (Paris, Études Cinématographiques, 1962)

Halliwell, Leslie: *The Filmgoer's Companion* (London, MacGibbon & Kee, 1967)

Haudiquet, Philippe: *Nouveaux Cinéastes Polonais* (Lyon Premier Plan, 1963)

Kracauer, Siegfried: *From Caligari to Hitler* (U.S.A., Princeton University Press; London, Dennis Dobson, 1947)

Kyrou, Ado: *Luis Buñuel:* (New York, Simon & Schuster, 1963)

Malerba, L., and Siniscalco, C. (Ed.): *Fifty Years of Italian Cinema* (Italy, Carlo Bestetti, 1954)

Messel, R. P.: *This Film Business* (London, Benn, 1928)

Neergaard, Ebbe: *Carl Dreyer* (British Film Institute, 1950)

Ramsaye, Terry: *A Million and One Nights* (New York, Simon and Shuster, 1926, reprint Frank Cass & Co., 1964)

Sadoul, Georges: *Dictionnaire des Films* (Paris, Éditions du Seuil, 1965)

———, *Dictionnaire des Cinéastes* (Paris, Éditions du Seuil, 1965)

Slide, Anthony: "From Manger to Cross," article in *Vision*, Summer 1967.

Taylor, John Russell: *Cinema Eye, Cinema Ear* (London, Methuen, 1964)

Wood, Leslie: *The Miracle of the Movies* (London, Burke, 1947)

Wagenknecht, Edward: *The Movies in the Age of Innocence* (University of Oklahoma Press, 1962)

INDEX

Principal Film References